MW00811436

Car Repair

Basic Auto Care and Repair Manual

(The Best Way to Do a Simple Car Repair Yourself at Home)

William Scoville

Published By **Andrew Zen**

William Scoville

Car Repair: Basic Auto Care and Repair Manual (The Best Way to Do a Simple Car Repair Yourself at Home)

ISBN 978-1-998038-88-6

Legal & Disclaimer

Upon using the information contained in this book, you agree to hold harmless the Author from and against any damages, costs, and expenses, including any legal fees potentially resulting from the application of any of the information provided by this guide. This disclaimer applies to any damages or injury caused by the use and application, whether directly or indirectly, of any advice or information presented, whether for breach of contract, tort, negligence, personal injury, criminal intent, or under any other cause of action.

You agree to accept all risks of using the information presented inside this book. You need to consult a professional medical practitioner in order to ensure you are both able and healthy enough to participate in this program.

Table Of Contents

Chapter 1: Before You Start Driving - The First Things To Do

Before you even begin riding, you need to ensure that your car or truck is sound and the entirety is in taking walks order, appearing its right feature and your car is in particular state of affairs. Just like your frame, you need to ensure that your car is that its foremost and first-class universal performance or health, and equipped so you can get on the street.

Even in case you're truly going a few block away, do a seen inspection of your car. This is a manner to make certain that you're making sure not something has ran into your car or that if a person has parked close to you that they failed to by chance recognize out a tail mild. By doing all of your visual inspection, you could ensure that you're not lacking some factor pretty simple that might sluggish you down on

1

the street. For instance permit's anticipate you begin using and additionally you in all likelihood did not understand which you were leaking antifreeze the whole manner down the road. You may not have a look at it however now you are out on the highway you do no longer have air con your antifreeze leak out and it is a warm summer time day. You can avoid a experience to an car restore store that is probably overpriced and rate you extra, via making sure you've got got sufficient antifreeze. You won't have leaks you do no longer comprehend about and you may moreover upload antifreeze fluid yourself.

Another place which you need to appearance out for, if you're ever pulled over at the thing of the street due to the truth you need safety for your vehicle and you've got referred to as AAA for example, make sure you find out from your AAA operator agent, the decision of the person they are sending, and get an define of their automobiles. What you do now not need to have show up is for a random person to tug over, and say that they're from AAA, and feature them tow you in which you do not need to move. Just ask them wherein they'll be from to make certain you aren't getting a tow from each other business enterprise. They may also take you to a neighborhood repair save and bill you for the towing issuer. AAA from time to time of their plan allows without price towing, however if the incorrect man or woman choices you up, you will want to pay the invoice. So be looking for this scam, as once in a while people try to do that, as a manner to get money, due to the truth they may say that they'll be from Triple A, however even as you get another time to the restore middle, it is after they explained that they have been with a one-of-a-kind company, and they will lie and say that they never instructed you they were from triple AAA.

Also maintain in mind that with any used car you need to do those inspections in advance of time if you may in advance than shopping for the car. You do not want to get a car home and suppose that you made this exquisite sound funding, only to discover that each one of the unique substances within the intervening time are two decades vintage and the whole thing desires to be replaced which include the battery the engine and the transmission! Try to test each place that you can and make a list of what may be vintage, terrific and deductible. Sometimes if you display a functionality vendor that you recognize your stuff, you can get a higher deal on a used vehicle!

Jacking Up Your Vehicle

You can preserve hundreds of coins doing all of your very own safety and protection, but one issue you do not need to scrimp on is jack protection. If you enhance your vehicle yourself, buy 4 quality 2 to 3 ton jack stands, and an first-rate floor jack. Always park your car on a flat surface earlier than raising it up. Rock the car earlier than going below it - in case you're afraid to do rock the auto, you want to be afraid to move beneath it. Have techniques to help a vehicle concurrently; in no way do not forget absolutely one approach. When the automobile is on jack stands and you are casting off the wheels, vicinity the wheels beneath the automobile as extra insurance in case of a jack failure.

Look at your automobile manual to decide the excellent factors for putting jacks - there are special convey factors and help places for everyday passenger motors and

SUVs/trucks. Before jacking, set the parking brake and chock the rear wheels.

If you're going to take away the tires, loosen the lug nuts on the identical time as the car is on the ground. If you loosen the lug nuts whilst the automobile is jacked up, the wheels may also begin spinning.

Tires

Rotation

Depending on how a whole lot weight you convey in the decrease once more of your vehicle or truck, your tires want to be rotated every 7,500 miles or six months, whichever comes first. If you do not need to jack up your automobile, the tire keep might also moreover moreover offer loose rotation.

Check the air stress in your tires monthly with a meter. It is IMPOSSIBLE to as it must be test out tire strain with a seen inspection. Air may be slowly leaking out of a small hollow that has been partially sealed, or leaking out the tire valve. The accurate air pressure for tires may be found within the owner's manual or on tire gambling playing cards placed on the point of the car door. Recommended air strain for the the the front tires can be extremely good than recommended air strain for the decrease lower lower back tires.

One issue that can be confirmed with a visual inspection is bubbling within the tires. A bubble looks like a small (or huge!) distortion in the tire - it will probable be apparent, like a ripple. A effervescent tire is not designed to be driven on, and may have a catastrophic failure resulting in what is euphemistically referred to as "fast air loss", or a blowout. In a blowout, the tire becomes shredded and flys everywhere, causing harm to the automobile and lack of control.

If you're converting a tire within the concern, try to find out the flattest place viable. Get as a protracted way a long way from the road as feasible; it isn't constant to exchange a tire on the shoulder of the street, so avoid this example if you can!

Replacing a Single Tire

It is proper for all tires on a automobile to have similar tread size and put on. Unfortunately, in actual existence a single tire can be punctured or destroyed with the aid of hitting a lower.

In this case, it's miles permissible to replace most effective one tire on the car.

On extra latest vehicle fashions with all-wheel pressure and balance manage, one new tire may additionally additionally furthermore probable interere with traction manage structures - test collectively together with your mechanic or proprietor's guide to be secure.

The tread at the contemporary tire can be shaved all of the manner down to wholesome the vintage tires. If you buy the tire from a tire hold, the store can diploma present tread at the ultimate tires and adjust the contemporary tire to fit.

Tread Wear

The tread on a tire is usually in touch with the street and permits the automobile grip the driving ground, this is crucial in rain or snow situations. Tire tread often wears down over time; a tire can be drivable however with low tread may be unstable.

One of the primary problems with low tread tires is the chance of hydroplaning. One of the functions of tire tread is to transport water across the aspects of the tire to growth the amount of ground area touch some of the tire and the street. When the amount of water on the street will increase past the tread's ability to disperse the water, the car may be riding on a cushion of water in choice to the road. When the automobile is now not touching the road, some of the property you are acquainted with doing to manipulate the car will not paintings. The satisfactory trouble to do is take your foot off the accelerator till your tread will become practical yet again.

Most modern tires have tread bars or tread placed on symptoms. A tread bar is a horizontal bar of rubber this is recessed and now not a part of the tire pattern. When the tire tread is flush with the tread bar, it's time to exchange tires.

An vintage-school way of checking the tread is to use 1 / 4 to check tire depth. If you can see the top of George

Washington's head, it is time to get new tires.

A word of caution - minimum jail intensity or sporting your tires all the way all of the manner proper down to the tread bar does not usually imply steady. Tires can slip in horrific weather, and as you are slipping and sliding down the road, physics will not be capable of pay attention you as you shout out, "There have become sufficient tread inside the tread bar!" If there's any query, and it is inside your price range, exchange them out.

Traction

All motors have axles, a the the front axle that holds the the the front tires in region and a back axle that holds the back tires and this is whilst Jake understood what he meant and the phrases sunk in. In wonder, he realized, he broke axles! When he went to have the Jeep repaired, the mechanic gave him a legitimate piece of advice. He described to Jake that his car grow to be too light. Jake had by no means heard this earlier than. He had audio device within the decrease returned so he knew that he delivered a few extra weight. No, the mechanic described to him, what you had to have with sandbags and Jake then remembered hearing a few problem about this in advance than however he did now not be aware of it. The sandbags or maybe firewood in the trunk function a reasonably-priced manner to weigh down a automobile inside the decrease again if it have end up slight. This is some thing it certainly is usually endorsed to individuals who own motors and vans which can be mild weight, basically although, with vans like Jeep Wranglers, that don't have plenty of weight within the lower returned of them. Lesson determined out for Jake. Either order more audio machine, or get invest in sand luggage and firewood and get an area that has a fireplace!

Chapter 2: Windshield Wipers

Changing windshield wipers is and clean and frequently overlooked maintenance item. The advocated renovation interval for wipers is six to three hundred and sixty 5 days, however in line with the National Highway Transportation Board, windshield wipers are only modified each 30 months on commonplace. If the wiper blades are damaged or cracked, they might scrape in competition to and damage your windshield.

On a regular foundation, take a moist towel and run it over the windshield wiper blade. The windshield wiper is a rubber cover over a steel blade; dust, dust, dust and bugs will boom at the wipers through the years. Wiping off the blade will increase its lifespan and offer you with an opportunity to look at the blade for worn or rigid regions.

If you live in an area of extreme bloodless or excessive warmth, freezing temperatures could make your windshield wipers hard and brittle. The warm sun can warp the rubber cowl and prevent a easy sweep of the wiper in opposition to the windshield.

When you're changing the windshield wipers, hold in thoughts to test the windshield wiper fluid stage.

Windshield Wipers Repair and Windshield Repair

If you have any troubles collectively with your windshield wipers, like in case you pay attention a squeaking noise that sounds nearly like steel hitting or scraping glass that is an indication that your blades are awful which means that that you want to have them changed. You can have a look at or the rubber on the blades and in fact take the quilt off that cover the plates.

You do not want a mechanic for this, but you do want to recognize what length blades you have in case you are going to exchange the blades your self. Replace the blade covers your self by way of manner of taking the blade covers to an vehicle elements hold and get new blade covers. You can also order those on-line and get them at a reasonably-priced price if you understand the version range. Just ensure to update them after they start to pass horrible. Once changed even though, in case you despite the fact that concentrate that metallic scraping sound, it could be an instance that your blades themselves want to be reset your automobile mechanic or technician can do this.

If you are visiting and in advance than large street trips, you want to make certain that you have checked each fluid degree and finished routine upkeep to your automobile. Fluid degrees are critical to the taking walks of your engine and assisting you get from detail A to factor B. When you journey on a huge avenue journey it is simpler and it is better to test ahead of time, than to wait till you get on the motorway have a stall out and feature an twist of fate or emerge as being at a relaxation area may you can not restart your car, only to find out that you need to visit an automobile repair preserve there wherein it might cost you more money in the end.

In the wintertime, make sure to go away your blades recognition as much as make certain they do not freeze toward the glass because of the truth if you celebrity to run the wipers, you could pull at the mechanism and this will motive them to now not work nicely and result in a steeply-priced visit to the mechanic. Make sure to de-ice your windshield and chip any ice away with a de-icing pick out that will help you to look on a cold and icy day. As the warm temperature reasons the ice to melt and the engine heats up, this will also help your wipers to thaw out and make them a whole lot much less complex to run.

Also make certain that in conjunction with your windshield that you don't have any chips on your windshield because of the fact a tiny little chip in change into a crack and then this can result in you needing the windshield repaired which can fee hundreds of greenbacks however a tiny little nick can be repaired at a quite low rate in case you seize it beforehand of time. Keep in mind, that you could get pulled over for small nicks and cracks in your windshield and you can attain a charge tag for having a cracked windshield, so get it repaired as fast as you may.

Lights

It's an notable idea to walk round your car every now and then to verify headlights, immoderate beams, turn lighting fixtures, brake lights, risks, and contrary lighting fixtures all feature nicely. On present day motors there are signs at the dash if a number of the ones factors are not running; however, it's miles possible for the ones signs and symptoms to be broken.

One anomaly to be privy to is that if one flip slight is flashing greater speedy than the other. This can be a hallmark of a blown fuse.

When converting light bulbs in the vehicle, if the bulb is a halogen bulb, keep away from touching the bulb with your hands. In a halogen light, the grease and dust out of your hand can motive the mild to grow to be dramatically warmer on the areas you touched. Uneven heating will affect the durability of the moderate bulb. Only manipulate the base of the mild on the same time as converting, or put on gloves to avoid contaminating the slight bulb.

Dash Lights

Check Engine Light

Modern motors (synthetic after 1996) have a gadget known as "On Board Diagnostics 2", or OBD-II. This machine robotically video display gadgets the most additives and man or woman emission controls of the engine.

When the device detects an anomaly, the check engine mild comes on. The take a look at engine light can suggest hundreds of severa things, however is constantly due to way of OBD-II. The trick is translating "take a look at engine" to the real trouble detected by using way of way of OBD-II.

The most commonplace motive for the check engine mild is a free fuel cap. The fuel tool for your vehicle is meant to be sealed. If the fuel cap is slightly ajar or has not been tightened until it clicks, the fuel tool will no longer pressurize and OBD-II will fireplace. Retighten the gas cap first and notice if the take a look at engine moderate is going off.

One weird trouble to appearance out for is mice or rodents in the engine chewing through wires. Check for mouse nests or gnawed wires.

If it isn't the fuel cap or rodents, there are more than one techniques to decipher take a look at engine. A respectable mechanic need to be capable of be part of a reader in your vehicle and tell you what errors code is triggering (free of charge!) You also can buy an OBD-II reader, or buy an attachment for your mobile phone which will connect with your ODB-II over bluetooth and can help you check your vehicle records proper away for your cellphone.

Chapter 3: Service Engine Light

The carrier engine light is each set on a timer based at the odometer, or analyzes some elements of the engine to determine whilst it's time to change the oil or get safety completed on the engine. This mild may be manually reset.

Brake Lights

The brake moderate will have a couple of meanings. In some automobiles, it may propose the parking brake is on; in special cars it could suggest to check the brake fluid. If the anti-lock breaking lighting are on, there can be a sensor malfunction or there can be a critical hassle with the ABS device. Definitely supply the auto in to a mechanic for an ABS hassle!

Batteries and Alternators

The vehicle battery serves some distinct features. First, it is able to offer chemical energy to the starter, to begin your car. It additionally stabilizes the voltage to your automobile to preserve it taking walks effortlessly. A lead acid car battery can be volatile to art work with because it consists of sulfuric acid. Once the auto is commenced out, the chemical response that brought on the ignition is reversed through the alternator on the equal time due to the fact the engine is jogging, placing the battery returned in it's far real condition. The alternator offers electric energy to the automobile as quickly as it's miles strolling.

Car batteries, like normal patron batteries you may buy at the store, have an expiration date, and the expiration date is nearly continuously late. If you've got got any questions on the capacity of your battery to keep a charge, you could take it into an automobile preserve and they may check the battery freed from rate. The current-day nation of battery manufacture isn't properly; many batteries will fail earlier than their listed lifespan.

The first symptom of a failed battery is that the auto will not begin. If this takes place to you, it is able to be possible to start the auto thru deactivating all the digital gadgets. Turn off the radio, headlights, outdoor and internal lighting fixtures, heater, windshield wipers, and so on. Attempt to begin the car all once more. You also can moreover want to smooth the battery.

To easy the terminals of a vehicle battery, you need to apply a base to neutralize any acid that has leaked out of the battery. A commonplace consumer base is a mixture of baking soda and water. In the sector, you can use a moderate acid collectively with coca-cola to clean a battery.

If the auto will even though no longer begin at this segment, you can attempt soar beginning the auto with a portable soar starter or jumper cables. Once the car is started, run it for about half-hour to recharge the battery. If the battery will not hold a fee, the battery or alternator might also moreover need to be replaced.

There are a few smooth exams to look in case your alternator has a hassle. Get your car started out, and unplug the excessive excellent battery terminal connection. If the automobile stops, the alternator isn't walking successfully; at this component within the startup cycle the auto have to be pulling energy from the alternator. Another exams are your lighting - if the dashboard or indoors lighting run brightly while the auto is accelerating, and dim at the same time as the car slows down, you've got alternator problems.

Fuses, Filters and Spark Plugs

If you do a seen inspection of the internal of your automobile, you can discover that you are missing a moderate interior, like one slight in your dashboard could now not work, or a moderate within the decrease lower lower back of the auto that doesn't slight up. These are simple matters that you could update with the useful useful resource of just converting and solving them yourself for a small sum of money. You also can change fuses if a mild is out. You can take a look at these with the aid of searching alongside the using force aspect door for a container it virtually is typically discovered along the door or the ground of your automobile and you can visit an car repair store and get the fuses on the right sizes with the aid of checking your proprietor's guide. This will assist you pick out out the right length fuses that need to get replaced. Try to undergo the owner's guide as soon as you get your car to help you find out where the whole lot is located. By information what fuses you want, you could make a list and choose up some extras at your community car factors hold, or hold your cash and get them organized online.

You can also keep extra fuses to your emergency kit. Because you have had been given a trusty once more up emergency package deal deal in your trunk you may be capable of have a flashlight that will help you if you discover that a fuse has blown and also you need to sense along the cause pressure element for the field to update it.

Another region that you may want to have a examine is to invest in spark plugs. You can purchase spark plugs to hold on your automobile however you may additionally genuinely make sure that you exchange them periodically. Maybe look at converting them every 30,000 miles or so but spark plugs can typically final 90 to one hundred thousand miles so just be searching out due to the fact in case you purchase a used automobile for example you cannot recognize at the same time as the spark plugs have been ultimate modified.

An area that you might possibly want to check into is to trade the filters for your vehicle. You can also moreover have cabin air filters that have to be modified or you could have engine air filters that make it grimy gritty and grimy and those also can need to be repaired and changed you may find the ones at your network restore save.

If you are up to it, you could change the clean out for the oil, however it can be simply as smooth to have it completed by means of a professional mechanic. Check the paper for oil exams that are on sale or discounted and keep your self time and money. You can be inside and outside in a few hours on a Saturday morning or in case you call earlier and find out what day is quiet and sluggish, you may pass all through the week and shop yourself from having to wait in an prolonged line. While you're there, stock up on the necessities you could want in your emergency package cited similarly within the studying.

Antifreeze/Coolant Levels

The words antifreeze and coolant can be a chunk deceptive, mainly for the motive that same liquid can be referred to as coolant or antifreeze!

Antifreeze has each a lower freezing factor and a higher boiling point than water. The antifreeze acts as an insulator, developing the sensible temperature variety of your engine. In the wintry weather, if you live in a cold area, antifreeze continues liquids on your engine walking at a colder temperature than they might typically - it stops the engine from freezing up. In the summer time, antifreeze increases the boiling thing of water in the engine so your water will not evaporate as speedy. The antifreeze cools the engine and consists of warmth from the engine to the radiator. Antifreeze furthermore acts a lubricant for moving parts which includes the water pump.

Only alternate antifreeze at the same time as the engine is cold. If the car has sincerely been taking walks, you can burn or crack your engine block, or heat coolant can injure you. If the prevailing coolant is dirty or discolored, drain the coolant and flush with distilled water in advance than inclusive of new coolant. There are severa one-of-a-type colours of coolants, so clearly as it's orange does not suggest it is grimy.

Overheating Issues

Every now and then you could discover that your car will start to run warm. What this indicates is that the engine is beginning to run hot and you could absolutely see the temperature gauge bypass up inside the automobile. What you need to ensure of is that after your vehicle is taking walks idly, which means whilst it's far sitting and on foot with the engine on, the temperature isn't going up indoors to a volatile diploma. If it does, which means that that there may be an hassle with the engine that desires to be addressed.

These are a few tips that you may use as you need to make certain you assume what might also furthermore need to be finished and try to study a ordinary list of checkpoints to ensure that your vehicle or truck runs resultseasily. For example if you're the use of down the motorway you need to make certain that you do not journey with the automobile taking walks warmness for too lengthy or which you do not stay in a low gear too much if you're dashing if you're going at a excessive fee of pace. Maybe you've got were given ridden with a person who may additionally want to flip off their engine at a forestall moderate as a way to prevent overheating. We do not recommend this. When your automobile is overheating, it wants to be serviced. Keep this in thoughts if you begin to have problems. You may additionally want to take it in to have the trouble assessed, however try and get a unfastened estimate which may not price you a few detail and could permit you make a decision honestly how a whole lot you in all likelihood may additionally should pay. Overheating problems and transmission issues are some of the most crucial reasons humans visit mechanics and occasionally the maximum pricey due to the fact engines are very steeply-priced to restore and update, but there are options. You can paintings together together with your mechanic or frame keep to find out a cheap opportunity, to rebuild your transmission and use older additives, and to fast repair it. Just do no longer be afraid to invite them and they may tell you. Sometimes an antique clunker is deserted because it's greater high priced to repair it and just much less pricey to get a greater recent clunker!

Why do I need antifreeze? Antifreeze is genuinely what it looks as if, it's miles an agent that acts as a manner to prevent your engine from freezing in cold temperatures. You do want to make sure that you have antifreeze for your vehicle at all times, even the summer time months anti-freeze need to be stored and saved on your trunk in a field like a gallon jug jar that you could purchase at the automobile shop, and you could shop a bottle in your trunk or perhaps a half of bottle if you're concerned about sporting these fluids spherical with you. The benefits of retaining antifreeze, is that during case you are ever out on the road and your antifreeze is taking walks low, you may store yourself money and time as an alternative of having to visit an car restore store or a body preserve. By having antifreeze with you, you may add it for your car your self in case you see your stages taking walks low.

Chapter 4: Checking the Oil

Although it's miles continuously crucial to test your manual, in wellknown, the exercise of changing oil each three,000 miles is actually too frequent for current vehicles. A trendy c language in recent times is 7,500 to 10,000 miles, and some vehicles handiest advise an oil change each 15,000 miles. Know your car!

Make superb your car is on flat ground earlier than you test the oil diploma. Depending at the make of automobile, the oil degree also can need to be checked at the same time as the auto is warmth or bloodless. Under your hood, the dipstick looks like a small metal pigtail. Pull the dipstick out of its field and wipe the give up off.

Insert the dipstick lower again into its field and permit it bypass all of the manner another time to the bottom. When you pull it out a 2d time, the dipstick will provide you with a popular idea of the oil stage. All dipsticks are top notch; a few say LOW and HIGH, some say MIN and MAX, some have an X. If the oil is below LOW, MIN, or the X, it's time to characteristic more oil.

The colour of the oil moreover gives valuable clues approximately what is going on for your engine. Brown or black oil is ordinary. A mild, milky oil can also additionally mean coolant is leaking into the engine. Any debris inside the engine oil also can advocate physical engine damage. If the oil has no longer been modified for a LONG time, it could be thick and gummy, or a black live comes off on your arms. This is a few other indicator that your oil wants to be changed; you do no longer need this dust walking thru your engine.

Sadly, a few greater moderen automobiles do no longer have dip sticks. They had been modified with digital gauges which simulate a dipstick. In the event that you have an digital gauge, your warning light want to go off to will let you apprehend that the oil wants to be modified.

When you are converting your oil, DO NOT overtighten oil drain plugs and filters! Make high quality that the gasket on your new oil clean out does not fall out of its groove while you are tightening it, in any other case the new oil will drain out at the same time as you begin the car. The corollary is, remember to get rid of the vintage gasket from the engine; a double gasket can spray everywhere, whenever.

Bumps in the Engine

Routine protection is some trouble that you want to make sure you take a look at whenever you get into your car. Because it has to do with protection, you usually want to make sure which you're driving your automobile down the road or toll road and its in maximum pleasing state of affairs. It does now not count in case you're truely going to the neighborhood keep, or if you're taking location a rustic street trip with a purpose to take you out of city for severa days, you want to ensure that the work that you perform in your vehicle and for your engine will help preserve your service mild off, and maintain you and your circle of relatives steady and stable.

The other benefit to performing habitual upkeep, is to make sure which you hold cash and you do now not need to worry about sending your vehicle in for safety. By doing things like checking the oil often, you could discover in advance of time if the oil is low or without a doubt out, and you could maintain your self masses cash with the aid of no longer having engine troubles, engine knocking or more harm if you run out of oil. If you haven't any oil and the engine and it starts offevolved bumping, you may be making a completely high priced mistake. Don't allow this form of mistake fee you extra money on the restore maintain than it need to. Set a warning on your laptop or an alarm at 3-months or 6-months to make certain you cope with your car's desires.

When the take a look at engine mild is on, do not forget it, but make certain to take it in for habitual service, The transmission could probably appearance and sound first-class whilst you depart the residence, but you may get down the toll road, visit transfer gears and understand manner too past due that you'll have a expensive repair to your arms. Once you get on the highway, it can be too beyond due to begin thinking in case you have to have taken the auto in for that pesky service slight. Because it wasn't an emergency to you earlier than, the worst time to realize you have been incorrect is at the same time as your gears are stripped. Transmission problems can are available in remarkable office work and are notably high-priced relying on your vehicle type. To make certain you do no longer ought to be hit with some thing that at the low prevent might cost everywhere from $2,000 to $4,000, just make sure you take your vehicle in for recurring protection, have your fluids checked frequently and deal with your engine when it runs. If it bumps, take it severely!

Bumps can also imply that protection need to be finished in your engine that could prevent you from taking location that massive street trip. If you have got got engine issues, do no longer danger happening the motorway with what can be a terrible transmission, or you can make subjects worse and being out of metropolis, can also furthermore need to art work with a foreign places mechanic who might possibly fee you extra. Have the engine checked earlier than you leave and communicate on your mechanic. Don't experience embarrassed if you have to provide an reason for the noise or you may continuously permit them to take a look at energy your car to appearance if they listen it and may without trouble discover what's taking place.

Fluids and Pads

Brake Fluid

Try to maintain your fluid levels to make sure which you are staying earlier of the game as it relates to normal vehicle upkeep. For instance, look at and trade your brake fluid and don't forget about your brake pads. This desires to be finished each to a few years and can help to save you a few thousand bucks in the restore save. Changing your brake pads may not be important until you try and prevent at a mild or intersection and concentrate a rumbling sound. Maybe it started out as a squeak or squeal weeks earlier and also you disregarded it. Now it's far rumbling. That approach your brake pads are lousy and need to be replaced right away. In the destiny, attempt to preserve up with this and as speedy as you pay attention a mild squeak, have them changed to make sure they do no longer positioned on down and come to be costing you more money in the long run.

Transmission fluid moreover needs to be changed every few years and the more you try this on a routine basis and get yourself into a time table with converting fluids, the a good deal much less hassle you could have down the street plenty less problems with maintenance and the extra cash you keep. You won't see it as being a huge deal in case you take a look at the entirety on a regular foundation, but if your transmission is going up, for example and you are at the dual carriageway in a distant places metropolis, you will never neglect approximately standing in line prepared round with strangers and being hit with immoderate payments. Make positive to avoid this thru the use of maintaining your automobile within the fantastic form you can. Treat your automobile like your toddler and make certain it might not sincerely run, however it hums!

Windshield Wiper Fluid

Something else which you should hold in your trunk, to your emergency kit is windshield wiper fluid, and in case you do no longer have the room for this, you could constantly try a bit Windex in an emergency. But keep windshield wiper fluid as it does now not freeze within the wintry climate time and you may get a smaller bottle in case you can not match a larger one in the trunk. What you want to make sure is that during case you ever want to exit and clean off the windows, you've got a few trouble it simply is resultseasily available. Every now and then, you could have a storm wherein you want extra wiper fluid, or your stuck behind a truck it's miles spitting cement or debris. Also within the summer season months, with a few towns which have pretty a few pollen, the use of your wiper fluid is a want so that you can get a clean picture of the street in advance.

Winter Maintenance

Have you ever visible a person the use of down the highway and they had a pile of snow all over their car? It looks as if a frozen tundra or ice system blowing swirls of snow all around the highway. The faster they pass, the greater immoderate it gets.

They do no longer even realize that they may be driving an igloo down the road it is a humorous sight to peer, however it is also form of unhappy, and frightening due to the fact they may be posting a functionality hazard to exclusive cars spherical them, and they may be risking the risk of their car stalling out on them due to the fact they are engine might not to have warmed up in time to get at the dual carriageway. By ensuring that you complete easy everyday safety talents inside the wintry climate time on your automobile, you may make certain yourself that your vehicle will run well it's miles going to be warmed up, and you do no longer ought to fear about engine problems battery troubles, or some thing else that would slow you down inside the wintry climate.

When you cope with your car within the wintry weather time, you want to make certain you rid it of any particles or snow and cast off and ice, moreover, so that you can make sure that your car will run properly and characteristic higher one. One vicinity in that you want to ensure that you commonly check the usual regular is with snow and ice. When you exit to start your automobile in the wintry weather, supply it time to heat up. That manner start your engine and offer your car time to certainly heat up even as you permit the ice to thaw and you can do this with a de-icer or ice choose for you to will let you to easy the residence home windows and hood. You can pick up a cheap de-icer or ice choose out at an automobile element shop. Start getting the ice off of your car even as your car is warming up. Always supply it as a minimum 10-20 minutes to run in terrible, icy climate. This is some thing so that you can help your car down the road as you're no longer forcing it to run at the identical time as some structures are still cold or frozen. What you are doing at the same time as you're giving your vehicle a chance to warmth up is you're assisting to heat up the automobile, and this will help your battery to characteristic nicely. Because the winters may be hard on motors, make sure to hold jumper cables within the trunk as nicely in your battery in case you need it, but don't worry, you do now not need to maintain a further battery lower back there!

As you begin to get the ice off your car, ensure that you get the ice off the pinnacle of your vehicle as nicely, due to the fact in a few states it's miles unlawful to go away ice on your automobile and feature snow waft flow from your vehicle on to the cars behind you.

Chapter 5: Warning Lights and Gauges

Make high quality that with your automobile you recall about any caution lights. Sometimes a slight can burst off if your gas is jogging low, or in case your oil is taking walks low. Lights can also go off if you have an trouble with the engine that calls for paintings. Now at the identical time as it'd be extremely good for car agencies to create a moderate that reads 'Routine Service Due,' so we are able to forget about that, unluckily, we do not have that, so whilst the carrier mild is going off, it's far better to simply take your vehicle in to ensure there aren't any issues that want to be addressed.

These are very vital because of the reality from time to time it is able to propose that you want regular protection, however once in a while it could imply that there's a problem that surely wants to be addressed. Another place that you want to ensure you do not forget approximately it if your vehicle is overheating or in case your truck is overheating. You want to ensure which you be privy to the temperature gauge as this shows the temperature of the engine. That's now not the temperature of the automobile that you're seeing as within the climate inside the indoors, whilst you be aware that indicator cross as a brilliant deal as have a look at warmth, it certainly is a caution that your engine is overheating. This is a few issue that must be addressed with the useful resource of your mechanic. The one factor you do not want to do if your engine is overheating, it's miles to take a huge street revel in. This warning is an indication to let you understand that your engine is on foot warm. When you are taking massive avenue trips, your engine may be strolling warmness the entire time which you had been at the motorway. This is a few component which you want to avoid.

Other areas that you want to be aware of consist of making sure that your vehicle remains smooth. Because we adventure loads on the road in the wintry weather time whilst the provider trucks use road salt, we must make certain that we wipe and wash our automobiles off in our automobiles after a large snowfall to make sure the salt might not corrode away at your paint.

Emergency Kit

A properly-packed emergency package may be the difference among getting right once more on the road or looking for a tow truck. Like converting the batteries within the smoke detector, the emergency package is regularly neglected or forgotten about until it's miles desired. Make great to confirm on a everyday foundation that gadgets with expiration dates are though within their lifespan. Particularly clean to miss are batteries within the flashlight, consumable meals, and devices within the first-beneficial beneficial useful resource package deal.

Following are lists of gadgets to embody in a large emergency kit or a small emergency package deal deal if region is at a top rate for your automobile.

Large Emergency Kit

The massive emergency package may be stored in a cardboard field or a plastic discipline to your trunk.

•AAA or roadside emergency card

•Adjustable wrench

•Antifreeze

•Blanket

•Bottled water

- Brake fluid

- Extra fuses

- First-beneficial resource package

- Flashlight with glowing batteries

- Flat head screwdriver

- Granola or electricity bars

- Ice scraper

- Jumper cables

- Oil

- Pliers

- Phillips head screwdriver

- Pocketknife

- Roadside flares

- Roll of duct tape

- Roll of paper towels

- Some rags and a funnel

- Spray bottle with washing machine fluid

- Tire inflator

- Tire pressure gauge

- Triangle reflectors and flares

- Vise grips

- Work gloves or latex gloves

Small Emergency Kit

- Extra fuses

- First-useful resource package

- Flashlight

- Help signal

- Multipurpose device

- Oil

- Pocket knife

•Rags

•Tire inflator

•Two roadside flares

The Pros and Cons of Fix-A-Flat

Tire puncture sealants which includes Fix-A-Flat are convenient. Spray the contents of the can right into a tire via the valve stem.; the tire does not want to be completely flat, but should now not be close to everyday running stress. The liquid in the can well-knownshows the hole and seals it. The tire desires to be reinflated after Fix-A-Flat does its magic.

The aftermath of Fix-A-Flat is in which the issues get up. Fix-A-Flat does now not apprehend exactly wherein the hole in your tire is; as an possibility, it spreads out invisibly coating the entire interior of your tire. When the liquid is sealing the hole to your tire, it's also sealing all of the specific places for your tire that don't have a hollow, developing a difficult coat inside the tire that can not be visible. This indoors coat can disrupt the touchy balance of a tire, making the auto vibrate and making the tires placed on unevenly.

Fix-A-Flat is most effective a short solution, and the tire will want to be patched commonly. Flat tire sealant has a maximum lifespan of 50 to a hundred miles. When you deliver the tire into the shop, they'll should clean out the Fix-A-Flat sealant from the interior of the tire. Fix-A-Flat may also moreover create a dangerous immoderate-pressure surroundings within the tire, and can invalidate the tire warranty. Fix-A-Flat isn't intended for use on performance tires.

Help with Auto Repair

Lastly due to the fact there are such plenty of apps that you may search for which have techniques to help you with such things as reminders for oil changes and unique car routine maintenance which you want, attempt happening-line and seeking out the amazing apps in an effort to will let you with automobile preservation, or maybe services that could assist to ship reminders to you periodically of routine maintenance that desires to be completed.

You can also ask your mechanic or communicate to magazines like Car and Driver for guidelines and recommendations in ordinary automobile upkeep and assist with car maintenance because the intention is to maintain your vehicle on the right track for normal ordinary safety. Just like you can time table a bodily or cleansing, you want to address your car this manner to assist it perform at its outstanding for you.

When you begin looking into making plans to analyze how you need to repair your vehicle, there are positive recurring subjects that you have to hold in thoughts, which embody standard upkeep and trendy matters to look out for to make sure your car or truck is strolling at its nice, and you may shop on organization prices in advance of time and excessive bills through converting things like fuses, filters and batteries, and noticing changes on your oil, antifreeze and engine whilst you see caution signs and symptoms and signs and symptoms or lights going off.

What you may look for will depend upon the time of 12 months, so it can be difficult at the start to get organized and preserve song of the whole thing. When you first begin your car in the morning on a wintry weather day, for example, there are variations in what to search for versus a summer season day while the temperature is up and you want the air conditioning on. There are some new apps that you may need to check out along side a today's one similar to the Gas Buddy, Repair Pal, Car Minding, Honks, Plug Share, Dynolicious Classic, and Witness Driving. The gain to those apps is that whilst you are faraway from your vehicle, like at domestic or at paintings, you may get popup reminders to provide you with a warning even as your business enterprise dates are springing up and what regular maintenance you will in all likelihood need.

Chapter 6: The Owner's Manual

One of the number one regions that you want to begin addressing along side your car or your truck, is to ensure that you have examine the proprietors guide. Reading the owner's guide is critical due to the fact the proprietor's guide is a Bible of what's on your vehicle or truck and a manner to help to maintain it serviced, to preserve your records updated, and to make certain that you recognize in which the whole thing is placed. For example some vehicle owner manuals alongside facet a manner to sections and offer advice on upkeep. They additionally offer you with descriptive maps show you in which the entirety is located below the engine, They can also additionally consist of factors like troubleshooting ordinary problems that would stand up, or even things like in which to check off your everyday protection and you can furthermore have your provider technician on the restore preserve fill this data out, moreover. What we're concerning is a segment in which each time you get an oil exchange you have got were given an actual written breakdown in which you can write down the restore center you went to, the date, what the mileage have become, and who serviced your vehicle so you apprehend while the final time have become that your oil in fact checked and through the use of manner of whom. Keep your statistics approximately your proprietor's manual to your glove compartment together with your registration and usually deliver it with you. This way when you have any problems the least bit or any organization related issues, you may have a quite without a doubt to be had source with a view to can help you troubleshoot troubles together with your engine tires or what have you ever ever ever.

In the identical way you can go to go to a medical doctor for a routine checkup you do the same aspect collectively along with your automobile. You want to ensure that your automobile is performing inside the most most beneficial manner that it could. Because your vehicle cannot talk for you, almost reflect onconsideration on it as you'll a infant, in which you want to decide what the hassle is and try and cope with any habitual regions to make certain which you are keeping it in tip top scenario. If you had a little one you may ensure to area a coat on the infant in the iciness time. You might make sure that you could feed the little one and cover the infant and inside the identical token along side your car or truck, you want to paintings to make sure which you have finished such things as trade the oil, rotate the tires, and finished normal upkeep to ensure that your car does not react to you with coughing and sputtering on the same time because it stops in the center of visitors.

Some preservation assessments you can not usually carry out right away and you can want to have absorb your vehicle to a store to have it inspected or to have a leak checked out,. You may also want to prevent in to have matters modified there, on the facet of your serpentine belt or timing belts, to make sure that this is repaired and walking properly this must be used. This want to get replaced every 40 to 60,000 miles and it is something that your mechanic will assist you to with.

Finding Parts and Service

Make sure to maintain on line for the factors which you need. Sometimes you may get deals that you'll not necessarily locate within the vehicle repair save. For instance now and again a smooth out may be expensive in one save, whilst it is fantastically reasonably-priced in some other, or maybe cheaper in case you purchase it on line. Make high-quality to test considered considered one of a kind stores collectively with Pep Boys, Auto Zone, Advanced Auto, and SGP. By buying round, you may locate price savings on numerous products you want on your car or truck. Keep in mind that you want to maintain your charges down low, so attempt to test your car as a way to find out and remedy issues in advance than they show up. For example, you want to make sure even as you have a observe your paint pastime, that you are seeking out any chips or dings for your paint and make certain which you without hassle contact those up with a pen. You need you save you long time rusting from taking vicinity, and this commonly starts offevolved out with a very small region that grows. You also can find those little spots throughout the tires in which you'll have avenue salt developing off the decrease once more of the tires in the snow and up on for your automobile. Make positive to check your automobile regularly to ensure that you aren't starting to see rust damage in tiny spots and now not identifying it. When it's time to have your tires modified, became around, and balanced, ensure which you maintain round at good deal tire places. Sometimes a close-by Sears or Pep Boys also can have the organization you want and also you additionally want to make sure which you're getting the exceptional price possible. Sometimes in the course of the vacations, mainly round Christmas or New Years, whilst loads of companies and stores are having their big fee tag gadgets inside the market, a whole lot of smaller shops additionally need to draw in business business enterprise, because of the reality they realize human beings are looking for the holidays.

Be careful that you do not overspend on the equal time as you get a company completed and make sure you take a look at your agreement to make sure which you have the whole thing this is going to be completed and you could control to pay for it. Also make certain that while you're having work finished if the repair guy tells you it will in all likelihood be a positive fashion of hours try and get an estimate at the kind of hours to make sure he does not bypass over the allocated charged time that he payments you for. Keep in mind, you may shop round for a mechanic or body keep and they all rate diverse quotes, so attempt to go online for a issuer that has a four or five big name score. That manner you're assured that your mechanic is honest, might not rip you off or rate hidden charges and you may refer them to others. If you're uncertain of their recognition, strive Angie's List, Yelp.Com or you may test with the Better

Business Bureau or Google court instances about the agency to see its records with clients.

Mechanic

Selecting an impartial mechanic for the primary time can be scary. The hassle is which you're seeking out a topic count number expert in a topic which you're not an expert in! With an independent mechanic, you may pay barely extra, however you could usually deal right now with the proprietor of the financial employer. Independent mechanics are normally highly skilled and car fanatics, in evaluation to chain stores who're continuously looking for to upsell you on vain offerings.

Since we live inside the net era, Yelp, Craigslist, and the mechanics files on Car Talk. You do not constantly need to find a mechanic that focuses on your sort of car, so long as the mechanic is sincere.

One approach typically proposed for discerning genuine mechanics from lousy mechanics is to carry your car in for a easy repair that isn't wanted for your vehicle. If the mechanic expenses you for some thing, the mechanic is devious!

The hassle with this easy method is that it does not bear in mind the other individual's time. It takes a non-zero quantity of time for the mechanic or his worker to assess your automobile; if your car wasn't in his keep, he is probably operating on a person else's automobile. Your vehicle is taking on location inside the mechanic's save. You can be (and want to be) charged for the mechanic's time regardless of what.

Chapter 7: Tips and Suggestions for a Dependable Car

A car is a high-priced monetary funding, so know-how the way to hold your car in extremely good shape might also need to spare you loads of coins. In current day, the fee of proudly owning a car is a lot extra than severa people also can take shipping of as real with-- there may be the charge of vehicle insurance insurance, taxes, vehicle loan hobby, repair paintings, gas expenses, and the charge of the automobile itself. By adopting all or just a few of those car care mind, you may begin sparing a giant amount of time and cash.

Simply a chunk of time committed to analyze want to spare you destiny restore paintings and loads of coins. You do not have to be routinely savvy to come to be privy to general car troubles. You truly have so that you can make use of your senses of sight and scent.

Have a look around

Are there discolorations beneath your vehicle? Drips? They might not be an trouble; but, in case you see damp regions, it could be a sign of some issue even extra excessive. Which shade is the fluid you are seeing? Is it orange, blue yellowish green? Then it would issue to a radiator leakage, overheated engine damage, or a water pump which requires restore artwork. Leakages like the ones should be treated unexpectedly.

Black oily fluid or darkish brown can also issue to oil leakage. A bad seal or gasket must result in this form of leakage. These styles of repair work can cost plenty, so it's miles an first-rate concept to take your vehicle to a mechanic you bear in mind.

A purple oily area may additionally trouble to transmission leakage or strength steerage fluid leakage. In some instances, you'll see easy fluid, it's usually most effective condensation and sincerely not whatever to pressure over. If you word slight smoke originating from your wheel as you are using, it'd advise which you have a brake this is stuck, and also you ought to tug over. Any sort of smoke shows which you need to appearance a mechanic.

Use Your Nose

Do now not hesitate to fragrance round and spot if you may become aware of an problem collectively in conjunction with your car. In case you odor burned toast, it might be an electrical scarcity or burning insulation. Do no longer risk the usage of it. In case you smell a rotten egg scent, it is very likely the catalytic converter, and it is going to should be consistent.

A thick sharp scent is frequently a signal of burning oil. Take a look beneath the car to look if you can discover a leakage. You may moreover see a bluish smoke originating out of your automobile's tailpipe-- you need to have this tested ASAP.

In case you fragrance fuel after your car falls short to kick off, the engine might also have ended up being flooded. Wait a couple of minutes and attempt all over again. In case you still discover a fuel scent, you'll probable have a leakage someplace for your fuel device, for you to be unstable, so have your vehicle taken to a mechanic right now.

These easy guidelines are going to assist in informing you of a probable issue collectively in conjunction with your automobile that want to be resolved.

Chapter 8: How to Correctly Inspect Your Fluids

Part of maintaining your automobile in tip-pinnacle shape is to ensure you mechanically inspect your stages of fluids. As a rely of fact, tracking of these tiers is important to your automobile fitness. It's an great idea to take a look at your owner's manual. There need to be diagrams of the engine there which might be going to expose you wherein to test out all of the crucial fluids. It's a splendid method to get an concept of wherein crucial fluids may be determined. You can furthermore employ the internet to hold up images that would assist you.

Engine Oil

1. You'll find toward the the front of the engine a cap marked "Oil." Examine your oil with the engine off. Get rid of the dipstick

2. Rub the oil off with a rag

3. Place the dipstick back in

four. Draw it out and get your reading

five. There are going to be 2 marks at the dipstick-- most and minimal -- some issue in-amongst indicates that your oil is brilliant. Beneath the minimum, and also you need to consist of oil. In older vehicles, it's far an top notch concept to observe your oil each enormous sort of weeks. In more modern-day motors, test out as speedy as a month.

Transmission Oil

In case you've got an automatic transmission, you are going to need to find out a dipstick to examine your fluid level. It's generally decided towards the rear of the engine. There are numerous strategies for examining transmission fluids, which is probably determined in the proprietor's manual. For the bulk of motors, they need to be strolling, and the transmission has to be in park or unbiased. To get a real reading, the transmission need to be heated up, so take it for a brief strain to supply it as lots as jogging temperature diploma. Make positive to test this once a year.

Engine Coolant

You need to in no way ever open the radiator cap while the engine is warm. You might be splashed through the brand new coolant and undergo maximum critical burns. Most automobiles have an overflow bottler with enormous level markings. You must make certain your coolant is in among the ones markings.

Power Steering Fluid

Your car uses oil to assist with the electricity guidance. This liquid have to be inspected often. Typically it is examined at the pump; but, in a few cases, the reservoir is separate and an extended way from the pump.

Brake Fluid

The majority of the extra modern-day cars let you check the brake fluid levels with out ever looking to touch the hold close cylinder cap. There are markings at the side of the reservoir, figuring out severa levels. As you are disposing of the duvet, make sure that not some thing receives at the paint.

Windshield Washer Fluid

You are going to look the arena which incorporates the blue fluid this is first rate for retaining your windshield tidy.

Chapter 9: Important Summertime Car Maintenance Tips

Prior to leaping into the automobile and going out on that summertime experience, it's an notable concept to make certain your car is in a ready-to-move state of affairs. Besides, there is in reality now not whatever worse than resting on the problem of the roadway looking beforehand to a tow truck whilst what you speculated to do have become spending a day on the seaside.

1. Examine Your Fluids - Run your automobile for a couple of minutes, and after that, observe the oil. It need to be inside the good enough range and it must additionally be tidy in your dipstick. Oil switches are counseled at various intervals various from three,000 miles to 7,500 miles. Examine your owner's guide for the guidelines in your automobile. In case the dipstick is at the upload mark, you need to

include oil. Despite the mileage, if your oil is unclean, you want to bear in mind an oil trade.

2. Examine Your Windshield Wiper Blades - Excellent wiper blades are going to be a real gain all through summertime thunderstorms and rainstorms, that might take area with out plenty caution. Winter season situations will be predisposed to make blades hard and useless. Examine all of your fluid stages, in addition to wiper fluid to ensure all of the subjects are crowned up preceding to leaving.

3. Know Your Tires-- You must be aware about the perfect tire inflation. You want to discover this in your car files, tire documents, or at the tire sidewall. Then get your tire strain gauge and observe their inflation. The warmth of summertime is going to enhance your tire strain, so it is a wonderful idea to test previous to using a ways.

In case you're using with underinflated tires, you're risking a blowout, at the same time as a tire it simply is overinflated locations you in hazard of hydroplaning in wet climate situations. Appropriately inflated tires are going to decorate the overall overall performance of your gasoline through as loads as three%, so there may be a actual gain to ensuring you've got a take a look at your tires.

While at it, take a moment to test out the tire tread. Utilize a cent and stick it inside the gaps with the top face down. If you are capable of see the top, it is time for brand-new tires.

4. Go to Your Mechanic-- A mechanic go to is a first-rate concept previous to any long journey. Your car is going to require ordinary music-u.S.A.And ordinary clear out and oil adjustments.

5. Examine Hoses and Belts -- Look for heavy located on or splitting and replace what goals replacing.

6. Be Prepared-- Constantly bring an emergency set with you that consists of a number one beneficial resource package deal, blankets, air compressors, jumper cables, and it is furthermore a awesome idea to deliver energy and water bars.

Chapter 10: Winter Season Car-Maintenance Tips

Winter season brings alongside a whole emblem-new list of troubles in your car. The depth of the iciness season is based upon upon in which you live. While greater trendy cars need much less intervention from us humans, they although must need to be equipped for the wintry climate season. By executing all or some of those car care tips, you may start to conserve a great sum of money.

1. Watch the Tire Pressure-- Tire stress, goes to move down whilst the temperature degree drops. When you keep your tires correctly inflated, you will get higher gas economic device, and it's miles going to help closer to blowouts furthermore.

2. Maintain Your Fuel Tank Above One-Quarter-- On older cars, this became executed to guarantee that the fuel strains

did not freeze. While it does not take area as often with logo-new motors, it may however arise, so why now not assure that it does now not. Additionally, at some stage in winter season the use of, it's an first rate concept to be geared up if you grow to be being stranded.

3. Inspect Your Fluids-- Some of your car's drinks are impacted with the useful useful resource of wintry climate season situations. Take a few minutes to observe your car's cooling device, and each twelve months, you have to do a coolant flush. Cooling gadget failure is the primary cause for the engine-associated breakdown, that would result in high priced maintenance. You'll need to encompass antifreeze at a 50/50 ratio of water/antifreeze. You ought to purchase an antifreeze ball tester so you must take a look at out your ratios at some point of the iciness and embody antifreeze each time needed. Make certain

your windscreen washing machine liquid is crowned up with wintry weather season liquid.

four. Examine Your Battery-- Older batteries may additionally want to have a problem at some level in the winter season with the cold. Make extremely good your terminal posts do no longer have any rust because of the truth whilst the posts are rusted, it can render it harder for the battery to get the automobile going. When there can be pretty cold climate, the lifestyles span of the battery can be decreased. Lastly, make sure you constantly have jumper cables, in reality in case your battery dies.

5. Do an Oil Change-- Even in case your vehicle isn't quite due for an oil alternate, now can be a first-rate time to do an oil exchange. With older cars, lighter weight oil may be applied to keep your automobile's factors a good buy better

lubed sooner or later of the wintry climate season. More modern vehicles make use of lighter weight oil yr-spherical.

6. Change your Windscreen Wiper Blades-- Altering your wiper blades at the beginning of the iciness goes to assure they are emblem-new. Winter season wiper blades do a much extra challenge of pressing the slush off your windscreen and scraping the ice away.

7. Put Snow Tires On-- Winter season driving situations suggest that you want to have exquisite traction. Based upon what you strength and wherein you stay, snow tires are generally an extremely good monetary funding. In superb places in which snowstorm is restrained, you can break out with a strong all-season radial tire.

eight. Bring an Emergency Set-- Your emergency set ought to consist of cold-climate device like jumper cables, flares, hats and gloves, flashlight, and desired device.

Chapter 11: Tips to Prolong Your Car's Life
Maintaining your automobile within the fine condition indicates you can lower the expenses of repair paintings, and you may unwind since you recognize you can depend on your automobile.

1. Your Car Break-In Duration

You invested your difficult-earned coins in searching for your dream vehicle, so you desire to appearance after it in a manner that is going to offer you as many years of relied on shipping as viable. Here are positive matters to hold in thoughts as speedy as you are the happy brand-new owner of that car.

- Throughout the preliminary one thousand miles, you need to hold your pace below 55mph or 88kpm or whatever the producer indicates.

- Never ever permit your brand-new car be idle for prolonged durations both at some stage in the damage-in and finally of its existence. Idling does no longer ship out sufficient oil at some point of the engine.

- Throughout the smash-in, live easy of heavy hundreds, like trailer towing, for the duration of the destroy-in period.

- When rushing up, hold the engine beneath 3000 rpm for the preliminary couple of hours of your using.

2. Drive With Care Every Day

You have to pressure your car with care day by day, now not only at some degree in the harm-during periods.

- Throughout start-up, do not race your car engine, especially inside the bloodless, because it includes years of decay to the engine.

- You ought to no longer permit your car idle to warmth up the engine. Since the engine isn't always taking walks at top temperature levels, the gas combustion is insufficient, inducing an accumulation of soot at the cylinder partitions, polluting oil, and bad wonderful factors.

- Moving to impartial at crimson lights minimizes the stress at the engine.

- When it is exceedingly bloodless or heat, stay smooth of the usage of at excessive speeds or speeding up too all of sudden. This conduct results in the requirement for repair art work greater regularly.

- You need to extend your tire's existence via using cautiously. Expect posted pace obstacles and comply. Stay easy of short starts, stops, and turns. Do no longer burn rubber, stay clean of placing curbs, and stay clear of potholes.

3. When You are Stuck, Relax

When one turns into stuck, the initial response is to rock the automobile via going contrary, after which ahead, whilst moreover spinning the tires. These acts are all right for a simply brief time period, but, in case you are in truth stuck, name a tow truck due to the truth that the damage you may do goes to a long manner surpass what the price of tow truck goes to be.

four. Go Light With Your Keys

Does your keychain seem as it can be utilized as an anchor? All the ones keys dangling off the ignition area unneeded strain on the ignition, and that could bring about the ignition tumbler put on. It's best if you could have your ignition key separate, or on the minimum, make sure which you have the load on your keychain down.

five. Put inside the time to find out the very extremely good automobile coverage corporation

Regardless of approaches conscious you're, catastrophe must strike whether or not or now not it is in the form of a mishap, wind typhoon or damage-in. It is important that you understand that you have coverage insurance with a sincere employer it truly is short to settle your declare. Ensure the coverage issuer has an fantastic credibility for claim payout, and that they're diagnosed for being accountable.

6. How to Protect Your Car Throughout Storage

In case you can maintain your vehicle for a month or extra, it is essential that you prevent unneeded repair paintings and damage from occurring.

- Top off the fuel tank to save you/decrease condensation from having the capacity to accumulate in the gas tank. Include a fuel stabilizer, then electricity throughout the block to disperse it throughout the engine additives.

- To protect the automobile, wax and wash preceding to storing.

- Put a four-mil polyethylene drop material at the floors to characteristic as a vapor barrier.

- Disengage your parking brake to help with minimizing deterioration.

- Place your vehicle on jack stands. This goes to put off the burden of the tires and wheels.

- Disconnect and remove the battery. You might also need to positioned the battery on a trickle battery charger, or you could drain the battery periodically, with a touch mild bulb, and after that, rent a low volt battery charger to fee it.

- Utilize a rag to plug the tailpipe to defend toward damp air.

Your Car Interior

Your vehicle's indoors requires precise interest to stay looking as brilliant because it did whilst it got here off the manufacturing line.

- Park within the Shade-- A garage constantly provides the best region to park your vehicle, however, while a garage isn't always an preference, you could lower harm from warmth and UV sunshine via using parking in the coloration. In case there isn't always any shade or when you have grow to be a whole lot of bird droppings from parking beneath the tree, buy a automobile color to optimize your protection. This is furthermore going to preserve your car cooler.

- Clean the Interior-- Routinely rubdown the indoors whenever you easy your automobile. Dirt particles, abrasive beverages, and spilled fluids like soda pop can be harsh and result in damage. You need to smooth up utilising slight detergent and water. You need to additionally vacuum every time. You must rub the dirt from the sprint gauges and the lenses. Do now not administer excessive pressure, or it is going to result in scratches.

- Utilize Flooring Mats-- Flooring mats must guard your automobile's carpeting, specially in the course of the wintry weather season, whilst there may be salt, slush, or maybe dust. The waffle style mats do not slip, and they may be smooth to clean off and vacuum.

7. Protect Your Windows And Door Seals

Initially wash with water and cleaning cleaning cleaning soap, then employ a rubber protectant together with Armor All ® or a silicone-primarily based definitely product at the doors and domestic

domestic home windows to preserve them conditioned and to prevent them from drying. You want to never ever hire an item this is oil-primarily based completely like WD-forty ®, that can damage your rubber.

In case your climate eliminating is making it viable for the water to drip into the interior, it is time to have it modified or steady. The majority of little leakages may be constant with a brush-on seam sealer. Fix torn element with a particular rubber caulking as a manner to be offered at most vehicle components shops.

eight. Stop Leather from Drying and Breaking

Leather interiors are abundant and prolonged-lasting, in case they will be saved correctly, however, at the equal time as not noted, they swiftly turn out to be being break up and unattractive. The leather-based ends up being stained with time. You ought to utilize a leather-based-primarily based cleanser to dispose of dust, and after that, comply with that up with a leather-based totally protectant which goes to face as much as discolorations, and keep your leather-based clean and flexible. It is moreover going to make it less tough to smooth up inside the future.

nine. Taking care of Upholstery

In case you have got got an upholstered interior, any automobile upholstery cleaner or residence upholstery cleanser may be applied. You will now not require a splendid deal as you do no longer want to, in fact, soak the material. Administer, and then rub off with a tidy cloth. In case the material has a sleep, utilize a brush to elevate the feel back up.

Using a material protector like Scotchgard ™ is going to aid the upholstery to stand as much as dust and reduce discolorations. It is moreover going to make it much less complicated to easy up the following time. Prior to the usage of a material protector, you ought to easy up the fabric.

To decrease the staining from youngsters the use of in infant seats, take a towel and located it underneath the automobile seat, or you may make use of a piece of heavy upholstery plastic.

Your Car's Exterior

- Shielding Automobile Paint From the Sun-- When your paint appears great, your automobile seems extremely good. However, at the same time as subjected to the solar's ultraviolet rays, it could begin to break the paint down and result in it to vanish. A garage is your preliminary line of protection; but, the bulk humans do no longer have a storage. The 2nd best element is to utilize a automobile cover, that can guard it from the elements.

10. Cleaning Your Vehicle

Cleaning your automobile makes it appear precise, but, it has a miles extra vital function, it's putting off the debris and dirt which could scrape your paint's floor. You must moreover easy your automobile sooner or later of the wintry weather season so the street salt, sand, and slush are removed in advance than they could harm your paint cease. It's awesome if you can go to a vehicle wash; but, it may be finished at domestic with a heat water bucket provided that the temperature level is higher than 0. Utilize a slight cleaning soap advanced for cleaning your car. At least a couple of instances a one year, you ought to make use of rim and tire purifier.

11. Waxing Shields Your Vehicle

Wax is critical to your vehicle's paint. It makes the paint seem logo-new, and it moreover decreases oxidation, and it produces a barrier which shields your paint from sap, contamination, chook droppings, and so on. Here's what to do to reap the proper safety:

- While fluid waxes is probably appealing because of the reality that you could get a very good glossy vehicle with lots much less paintings, the detail is that paste wax is greater powerful, tougher, and lasts hundreds extra. Try to discover a paste it genuinely is high in carnauba wax.

- Next, thru using a sponge, administer a surely skinny coat of wax to the paint. Ensure it is even, and do not take a look at it too thick (an everyday mistakes). If you practice it too thick, it is virtually tough to dispose of all of the residue.

A soft cloth works preferably to dispose of the dry wax. It will not scrape the paint.

- Due to the truth that the wax on the hood deteriorates quicker from the engine warm temperature, it's miles an outstanding idea to apply a further couple of wax coats.

12. Place a Brand-new Skin on Your Vehicle

Paint is inclined, however, there may be a way to protect the places which will be predisposed to get the most stone chips utilizing a self-adhesive urethane movie. These urethane movies are excellent whilst used professionally; even though, in case you are reachable at this form of difficulty, you can deliver it a pass for my part. 3M ™ and Scotchgard ™ are each actual picks. Once it is administered to the auto, you could wax and smooth as not unusual.

thirteen. Touch up Chips

Even as we're relatively-careful, chips appear. Touch-up paint is an opportunity, and for additonal trendy vehicles, it's far pretty easy to evaluate shades. Utilize contact up paint to touch up chips earlier than the rust is capable of begin to rust.

14. Quick Repair Work for Light Covers

In case you locate yourself with a broken taillight cowl or flip sign, you could change the entirety. You may additionally need to utilize tape for the repair, which is going to maintain you over earlier than you could efficiently restoration it. You need to utilize the crimson or orange tape this is produced for this. Others aren't going to stick.

15. Changing Bulbs Effectively

As you're switching out burnt-out bulbs, clean the dust away. In case the socket has surely ended up being rusty, employ a piece metallic wool or twine brush to easy away rust. Then rub away the debris and set up the alternative bulb.

sixteen. Fixing Little Chips in the Windscreen

Rock chips or fractures within the windscreen may want to prevent visibility, and even as left not noted, they'll be willing to get a excellent deal large whilst temperature stages change. It's lots more less expensive to prevent into the windscreen repair store and function a chip or fracture constant, which brings lower back the initial glass integrity and keeps clear visibility.

17. When Hauling on the Roof

You may be lured to load up your roof. Inspect your proprietor's manual in your car's specifications. It's generally someplace in between one hundred and fifty to 2 hundred kilos or sixty eight to ninety kg. What does that suggest? That's about eighteen 8' 2x4's or 3 3/4" plywood sheets. To defend the roof, you can positioned a blanket or a chunk of cardboard down. You want to moreover purchase a baggage rack set.

18. Fasten Your Load

Constantly ensure your load is installed to protect your automobile's paint from being dented or scratched. It will pay to buy the right cargo, motorbike or luggage racks. You need to furthermore make use of cargo straps and placed a blanket to start with to guard the auto's ground.

19. Examine your Wheel Well Splashguards

Splashguards are created to preserve slush and water from sprinkling up into the engine compartment doing damage to electric elements. Generally, these splashguards are as an possibility lightweight and are frequently peeled without the driving strain knowledge. You ought to have a examine those guards frequently, and in case they may be unfastened, refasten or update them.

Tires, Wheels, and Brakes

20. Look For Unequal Tire Wear

When tire inflation is preserved, and you still experience abnormal put on, it might suggest that you require a wheel alignment. It need to moreover advise which you have in fact been poorly the usage of your brakes, worn bushings, inner tire damage, marvel issues, or a bent wheel.

21. Inspect Tire Tread

Various worldwide locations have numerous requirements concerning tread. In The United States, all tires presented want to have "put on bars" formed into the tires. This renders it simple to apprehend while tires want to be lawfully changed. The easy guiding precept is that once the tread is worn proper all the way down to 1 1/16" or 1.Five mm, the tires should be changed.

22. Maintain Caps on Valves

One little piece may additionally need to spark off lots of sorrow. When the valve cap goes missing, it may bring about a leakage. These caps prevent wetness and dirt from coming into. Inspect your valve caps and make certain they're not harmed or missing. When you have got tires modified, ask the store to make sure the tires have logo-new valves.

23. Have Tires Properly Inflated

Ensure your tires are efficaciously pumped up. When tires are below-inflated, it induces intense anxiety and heat that would result in tire failure. To get the most life out of your tires, purchase a strain gauge to make certain which you are capable of take a look at your tires robotically. Once a month is generally endorsed, however, throughout warm climate, it must be executed greater often. For a precise studying, test while the car has definitely been pushed less than a mile and while the tires are cold. Inflate based absolutely absolutely upon the manufacturer's recommendations.

24. Do the Wet Thumb Test

As you're utilizing a provider station air pump, previous to pumping the air on your tire, depress the inflator valve pin together at the side of your thumb. You are looking for wetness. If your thumb in the end finally ends up being damp, enter into a provider station, and allow the personnel understand the tank have to be worn-out. Locate every different provider station. Why is this so essential? Well, because of the truth that if that wetness gets caught inside the tire, it could result in versions within the tire pressure, and it could furthermore rust rims.

25. Turn Your Tires

Routine tire turning enables to ensure that the tires put on out in addition, and it's miles going to result in the most suitable tire existence. Your initial rotation is genuinely essential. Your proprietor's manual is going to offer you with a rotation duration and sample. If you can't discover this schedule, then turn your tires each 6000 to 7500 miles.

26. Tire Inflation and Temperature Level

The temperature degree influences tire pressure. When the temperature ranges bounce or drop, your tire pressure is going down. With underinflated tires, they may be capable of put on quicker and reason terrible driving

27. Utilizing Wheel Cleaner

Your wheels take a pounding due to being in contact with the roadway. Mix that with brake dust, and you have have been given simply were given a few tough spots to cast off. Routine automobile wash cleansing cleaning soap without a doubt cannot get rid of this gunk and grit. You want to utilize a cleaner this is specifically created for discolorations. There are severa wheel cleanser formulation for severa wheel finishes like aluminum and chrome. You should moreover encompass a protection layer via making use of wax on painted wheels and wheel polish on metal wheels.

28. Lubricate the Lug Nuts

If you do now not periodically lube your lug nuts they're going to seize to the studs because of rust. Repair work might be costly, and when you have a blowout, you will probably discover your self within the requirement of a tow. Every time you turn your tires, it is an wonderful concept to utilize an anti-capture lube, which you can purchase at your nearby vehicle save. Utilize a twine brush to clean up the studs, after which use the lube. It's created to prevent lug nuts from seizing while concurrently stopping them from running their way off as you're the usage of. In case you do grow to be with a seized lug nut, strive squirting WD-40 or Liquid Wrench on the impacted lug nut. Wait 10 to half-hour for it to permeate. After that, employ your ratchet to cast off the lug nut.

29. Stop the Hubcap Loss

Hubcaps come to be being ruined, artwork themselves free, and may then disengage themselves out of your automobile. They can be expensive to change. You could forestall this from occurring via:

- Newer plastic hubcaps which might be held in spot through using way of a maintaining twine ring that you snap into the wheel tables. Be careful no longer to interrupt or flex these tables.

- When it includes the older metal hubcaps, pry the steel clips pleasant quite outwards. This have to address any problems.

- Utilize a rubber mallet and tap carefully as you move throughout the hubcap in a circle. Do not strike an excessive amount of considering you'll harm the clips.

30. Have a Routine Wheel Alignment

Wheel alignments are vital. When your wheels are not aligned because it need to be, your tires are going to wear down faster, you can have poorer dealing with, and it may result in wear to the pinion or rack or splendid steerage elements. Refer in your proprietor's manual for the recommended time desk, in any other case, at the least have your wheel alignment examined yearly. In case you've got a 4x4, otherwise you do a wonderful deal of off-avenue, have your wheel alignment inspected extra frequently. If your vehicle pulls to the left or right, have your wheel alignment finished.

31. Top Off Your Brake Fluid

You have to research your brake fluid month-to-month. Before beginning the master cylinder cover, rub away any dust. If you need to consist of fluid, test with the manufacturer's recommendations. You want to in no manner ever change liquids. For example, in no way ever utilize energy guidance fluid in desire to brake fluid. Never ever make use of brake fluid which were opened, due to the truth as speedy because it has actually been subjected to air, it is able to emerge as being polluted rapid.

32. Taking care of Your Anti Lock Brakes

The anti-lock brake device in modern-day vehicles is touchy to wetness, that could rapid harm the high-priced ABS pump and result in the interior of the brake traces to rot. Given that brake fluid have a propensity to attract in wetness every huge sort of years, your brake strains need to be bled. They are going to additionally be inspected if you have your every year wheel alignment test. If you've got got got a 4x4 otherwise you dedicate loads of time without work-street, have them tested more regularly.

Vehicle Engine and Related Systems

33. Examine Your Oil

This is substantially crucial!

- Begin by means of way of the use of draining your antique oil.

- Then tidy the drain plug on the oil pan, and easy it off earlier than re-installing your oil plan.

- To check out your oil, carry out your automobile for as a minimum 15 mins to make sure that the oil heats up.

- Park the automobile on level ground.

- Switch the engine off, look ahead to fifteen minutes in order that the oil is able to drain once more to the oil pan.

- Get rid of the dipstick and rub it till it is easy.

- Reinsert it and press it all of the way in.

- Once once more, yank the dipstick out and check the oil degree.

- It want to be somewhere in among the hash marks. If in the upload location, encompass oil based upon your manufacturer's specs.

34. Change the Oil

Today's manufacturers endorse an prolonged length in among oil changes, however the truth is that greater often abrasive dirt and metallic debris are taken out out of your engine, the longer it's far going to purr like a kitty. It prolongs your engine's lifestyles. If you choice to optimize your engine, are trying to find recommendation from the schedule for prolonged periods for your proprietor's manual. This is important in case you strength in save you-and-cross traffic mechanically. For numerous years it have grow to be suggested that your oil ought to be changed every 3000 miles. Those periods are growing, but, there may be no threat in adhering to the antique numbers.

35. Which Oil to Utilize

There are some of oils inside the market. Let's check them them.

- Detergent Oil-- Nearly all modern multi-weight oils are detergent oils, which cast off soot from the interior engine factors, and after that, keep those oil particles. These particles are too small to become being caught by manner of the usage of the oil filter, simply so they live drifting within the oil. This is why your oil remains darker. These debris do now not damage your engine. Nevertheless, while the oil finally ends up being saturated, it cannot maintain on keeping these tiny debris. Existing oil modification schedules take region earlier than this takes location.

- Oil Viscosity-- The oil viscosity is described via using utilising 2 numbers. The initial range is the viscosity at the same time because the oil is cold. You are then going to word the letter W located through every other quantity. The W represents "winter." The majority of human beings trust it way weight. Then, there is some other range, which informs you of the viscosity at the same time as the oil is at running temperature degree. The oil thickens as the amount grows.

- Climate Considerations-- Your owner's guide is going to phrase which oils are appropriate to make use of at various temperature ranges. For instance, in case you are living in a heat weather, 10W30 is the appropriate possibility to 5W30. Previously, there has been a summertime oil and wintry weather season oil. That's the case not. Nevertheless, if you are living in a warm weather, and you are utilising 10W30, then ensure you convert to 5W30 for the wintry climate.

36. Changing the Oil Filter

As you convert your oil, you're moreover going to regulate your oil clean out. It is superb to stick to what the producer advises for the clear out, but in some time furthermore specific filers provided via agencies like Pennzoil, Valvoline, Motorcraft, and masses extra. These filters are going to in shape the maker's filters. Remember that the quality of producer's filters is a extraordinary deal better than the marketplace filters.

There are additionally alternate emblem call filters, which might be placed at an entire lot of the fast oil trade locations. For folks that rent synthetic oil, pinnacle rate filters are generally implemented. They are pricier, however, the blessings have clearly been showed.

37. Changing the Fuel Filter

Recently makers have in fact been telling us that we do not need to meddle with our fuel filters so often. We although propose changing your gasoline filter out at least every yr. When a gas clean out turns into obstructed, it's far going to bring about your engine to carry out badly, and it's far going to lower your fuel mileage. It's moreover an example that a gas tank is beginning to rust. You are going to see the ones debris inside the clear out.

38. Enhance Gas Mileage with a Clean Air Filter

Inspect your air clean out each handful of months, and while it is unclean, change it. Air filters are easy to change. With a carbureted automobile, you simply get rid of the huge metal cowl. With gas-injected motors, you dispose of the rectangle-shaped field. Your manual goes to indicate to you precisely in which it's miles.

39. Have a Healthy Transmission

It is essential to adjust your transmission liquid after the initial five,000 miles in a emblem-new automobile, and after that, whenever your mileage is round 25,000 miles.

40. Never Ever Overfill the Crankcase

Do now not overfill your crankcase with oil, given that in case you do, air bubbles are going to shape in the oil, and after that, the oil pump isn't always going to have the potential to art work correctly. This may additionally need to result in an engine getting too hot and stress being positioned on hundreds of engine elements. It have to moreover motive fouled sparkplugs.

41. Remember Your PCV Valve

The pleasant crankcase air glide (PCV) valve is a part of the emissions machine in older cars. The valve's undertaking is to re-flow into in thing burned gases from the engine crankcase to the combustion chamber. It's pretty essential, and it need to be changed every 30,000 miles. It moreover assists in improving fuel mileage via manner of stopping the buildup of sludge and rust.

40 . In case You Tow, You Wish to Have an Oil Cooler

If you appoint your vehicle to tow a trailer of a few type, you need to have an oil cooler set up. You could probably moreover set up a transmission cooler. They are clean to set up, they do not price heaps, and spare you big dollars in phrases of transmission and engine upkeep.

40 3. New Spark Plugs Equate To Better Gas Mileage

Electronic ignitions, and vehicles with pc structures on board have simply gotten rid of the requirement for a recurring song-up. Nevertheless, it's far though crucial to exchange your spark plugs automatically. The majority of makers recommend converting your spark plugs each 30,000 to

40,000 miles. Excellent spark plugs resource your engine in carrying out plenty higher, and you can pleasure in higher gas mileage.

40 four. Inspect the Hoses

Hoses become being fragile and could smash with time. When the car is grew to end up off and has clearly cooled, pinch the hoses. If they may be as an alternative stiff, make a crunching noise, have bulges, are touchy or sticky, or appear collapsed in any detail, it shows the hose is fragile and want to be changed. You ought to in no manner ever strength with a compromised coolant hose because of the fact your engine may in all likelihood get too warm, and you may end up with a really high priced repair paintings invoice.

45. Belt Tension

You need to have a have a look at the belt tensions. You need to additionally look for located on. You'll discover belts which run your Air Conditioning compressor, water pump, and energy steering pump. To search for tension, push in the middle of the belt in which the lengthiest uncovered component is. In case you're able to depress the belt half" to at least one" or 13mm to 25mm, however no more than that, the anxiety is notable. Otherwise, you can each take your automobile to a automobile hold for a exchange, or in case you are gifted, you could do it in your very private. Look for fractures and fraying, which recommend that you need to alternate the belt(s).

forty six. Proactively Check the Timing Belt

Your manual is going to inform you while you ought to exchange the timing belt at 50,000 miles; however, it does variety. When a timing belt stops taking walks, it may cause countless bucks of damage to the engine, so it is perfect to be proactive.

47. The Engine Cleaning

It's a first-rate concept to carry out an engine smooth every handful of years. By doing away with all of the gunk and dust, it ultimately in the end ends up being masses lots less hard to look any leakages. When cleaning your automobile, preserve in thoughts no longer to soak vital engine components like electric factors or distributor caps. You ought to use plastic baggage to cover them. Liquid dish cleansing soap abilties efficaciously to lessen grease. There are moreover masses of extremely good grease-cutting detergents in the marketplace.

Car Battery, Air Conditioning, and Other Crucial Parts

forty eight. Switch Your Air Conditioning on in Winter season

If you count on I simply have in reality misplaced my mind, I surely have not. You ought to reveal your Air Conditioning on as a minimum a number of times in the iciness season to stop your Air Conditioning compressor from seizing.

49. Preserving Your Vehicle Battery

It is vital on your automobile battery to be in suitable form, and for this to stand up, you ought to do a everyday protection. Maintaining your vehicle battery isn't that hard.

- It begins with preserving your battery tidy. Rub with a wet rag utilizing mild dish detergent.

- Clean the terminals or battery posts -- first of all do away with the horrible cable, and then the effective one. Red = outstanding, Black = terrible. Soak a brass twine battery brush into water and baking soda combo. Only multiple tablespoons of baking soda included in a bit of water, and you may have the proper aggregate.

- Look for fractures on the battery itself. Additionally, look for bulging. These are caution signs and symptoms and signs and symptoms that the battery wishes to be changed.

- Re-set up your battery cables beginning with the brilliant.

50. Preserving Your Battery

In case a battery has a vent cap, you could desire to eliminate it and feature a study the electrolyte diploma. It has to cover the battery's fundamental plates by way of way of way of at least a half of" or 13mm. You have to not make use of tap water because of the fact that it could have minerals which may also harm your battery. Rather, employ distilled water.

fifty one. Sealing a Leaky Radiator

In case you have got a radiator which is dripping, there are a numerous radiator sealants which can be located in a liquid or powder shape. These items distribute through the radiator, and once they acquire the hole, the item receives in touch with air and creates a seal.

fifty . Water down the Coolant

Your cooling device desires to encompass water and coolant-antifreeze. You do now not employ undiluted coolant. Usually, the combination is a 50/50 ratio. You need to moreover never ever utilize immediately water in your radiator. Inspect your coolant-antifreeze as a minimum some of instances ordinary with month and ensure you have got enough insurance at some stage in cold weather to guarantee that your radiator does now not freeze.

fifty three. You Need To Flush Coolant

Coolant-antifreeze loses its overall performance and ultimately subsequently finally ends up being polluted. You have to flush your device each 2 years for sure coolants and each 5 years for others. Check out your coolant label for entire commands. In case you do not do a flush often, you run the threat of harming your radiator, and blocking off the heating unit middle. The water pump and thermostat also can stop going for walks.

54. Never Ever Blend Your Coolants

You have to by no means ever aggregate coolants of severa sunglasses. In case your coolant is purple, then do not embody inexperienced coolant, on account that in case you do, you will turn out to be with a dense goop answer which can not do its paintings.

fifty five. Inspect Power Steering Liquid

Each month you need to study your energy steerage fluid as soon as the auto has in fact heated up. If the amount is low, you must have the hoses and pump checked for any form of leakage. If the strength steering fluid is low, you can harm the power steering pump.

Chapter 12: How to Have a Healthy Fuel System

The gasoline system is crucial in your car walking efficiently. The gasoline machine affords the engine with the diesel/gasoline it wants to function, and if any part of the gas machine is not running as it have to be, it may cause first rate issues.

The Fuel Sending Unit

This is wherein gas is useful. The gasoline receives to the tank via the filler tube. There is a sending tool which sends out information lower again for your gauge regarding the amount of gas you have got. In case this sending unit ceases taking walks, you are not going to get a unique analyzing of virtually how a good deal gas you have. In case the gas gauge quits going for walks, the trouble is going to be each with the gasoline sending gadget or with the gauge itself.

The Fuel Pump

In the greater present day vehicles, the fuel pump is generally inside the fuel tank. On older vehicles, it is linked to the body rail or the engine. In case the gas pump begins offevolved to malfunction, your vehicle can tumble and run rather greater or less. If the gas pump falls short, your vehicle isn't always going to artwork. Many current gas pumps can be heard as you turn the ignition key. In case you do no longer pay interest the pump working and your automobile could no longer get going, it is probably your fuel pump.

Fuel Filter

A tidy gasoline filter out is essential for the capability of your engine and its existence span. Fuel injectors have exceptionally small openings that can abruptly emerge as being obstructed, so the gas clear out prevents the ones debris from making it via. If your automobile has high mileage, adjust the fuel clear out each 12 months. For emblem-new cars, take a look at the producer's commands. Indications of a blocked gas clean out embody the engine not starting or faltering at excessive speeds. This is the most normal problem with the gas device.

Fuel Injectors

Since 1986 the majority of home vehicles have in reality been gasoline injected. The gasoline injector is a small electric powered powered valve, it really is near and opened thru an electrical signal. Unclean injector office work in time as deposits slip by the gas filter. This ought to activate gas injectors to stick open, sending out immoderate gas to the engine, or they may be able to turn out to be being plugged, sending out inadequate gasoline to the engine.

Using a routine fuel device purifier assists in keeping the injectors easy and may be received at department shops, vehicle shops, and lots of filling stations. Place it in your empty tank and fill it after that. This is going to easy your injectors. Redo this each 3 months.

Where You Purchase Gas is Important

You is probably stunned to find out that it isn't critical in that you purchase your fuel. You must constantly buy from a properly diagnosed national brand call. Gas stations without any affiliation buy what is left on a truck while the day ends, and the mixture should make some automobiles run horribly. Additionally, any water within the fuel is going to result in your engine to run badly, and it is going to promote rust development for your gas tool.

When it relates to octane, growing the octane is throwing the coins away besides the automobile maker in particular advises it. You are not going to get higher fuel mileage or an entire lot better functionality. For the majority humans, the maximum low-price octane at the pump is all that the auto dreams.

Last Minute Fuel Tips

- When you park in the solar, you will experience gasoline loss due to evaporation, so park in the colour.

- Make effective you constant your fuel cap.

- When your cap is loosened, or absent, gasoline is going to evaporate, so make certain your cap is tight.

- Don't trouble rounding off your fuel tank. When the automatic nozzle clicks off, stop pumping, otherwise it's miles going to splash spherical and leak out.

- Effectively inflated tires issue to a whole lot extra gasoline mileage. Underinflated tires thing to inferior fuel mileage.

- Make sure your engine is tuned up. An effectively tuned vehicle can decorate your fuel mileage thru approximately 5%. A misfiring spark plug may additionally want to lower your gasoline typical performance via the use of as loads as 30%.

Chapter 13: Body Care Tips

Maintaining your car looking fantastic does no longer want to be hard. Even an antique automobile might also need to appear like brand-new one with habitual care. We have honestly all seen those collector automobiles that have by no means ever been repainted. Your automobile's paint should appear that remarkable years from now as nicely.

Cleaning Your Vehicle

Wash your car at the least one time a month. Bugs, limestone, chook droppings--they will all depart irreversible spots on your paint if not wiped clean off. The wetness hastily dries on a tidy vehicle; but, even as the auto is unclean, the wetness collects in the unclean places, that would motive deterioration. It's perfect to utilize a bathing object superior for the paint to your automobile.

At least occasionally, you want to furthermore utilize a pressure washer. The ones at the coin car washes feature successfully. The stress washer has the capacity to deal with dust in difficult places. Do no longer area the stress water very near the paint as it can set off peeling.

Waxing Your Automobile

Wax your car automatically. The wax makes your automobile lovable and easy, and it shields the paint from environmental elements, fading and discoloration. It takes clearly round an hour to wax an entire automobile. An excellent wax is going to remaining spherical 3 months. By waxing your automobile best four instances in line with 365 days, you could ensure your paint appears brand-new.

There are an entire lot of wax devices in the market. So many who it may be mind-boggling trying to pick out one. Staying with a carnauba car wax is a exquisite opportunity. It is easy to apply and holds up efficaciously.

How to Fix a Stone Chip

If you do no longer restore a stone chip in your paint speedy, it's far going to begin to rust. It's not as difficult as it would seem.

- Head to your company to suit a spray paint for your vehicle's paint color.

- Wash the auto and allow it to dry.

- Get your spray paint and shake properly.

- You'll moreover require a pointy timber stick.

- Spray a tiny amount into the cap.

- Soak the stick within the cap.

Chapter 14: Tips for a Good Automatic Transmission

Become Well Acquainted With Your Automatic Transmission and Have it Serviced

Your car transmission transports the engine electricity to the strain wheels utilising a sequence of equipment sets, bands and clutches. The transmission mind is the valve body, which reacts to every electric or hydraulic indicators which tell the transmission on the same time as to transport. The pump is the core of the transmission providing the hydraulic strain required for lubrication and administering the required amount of lubrication to friction devices. The transmission is the most complicated a part of your car's complete stress shaft. There are more than 1,000 shifting components, and every one wants to characteristic flawlessly for the following piece to run properly.

With a number of transferring elements, it isn't hard to understand why safety is so essential. Invest om normal clean out and fluid changes and evaluations, and you can spare countless bucks in repairs. There is actually not some thing low-rate about solving a transmission.

10 Ways to Extend Your Transmissions Life

1. Frequently look at transmission fluids. See the proprietor's guide for servicing details.

2. Examine the transmission liquid while it has sincerely been strolling heat. Stop and pass net page traffic, choppy terrain, hauling a trailer, and warm weather have to all bring about immoderate transmission warm temperature which can bring about the fluid loss, fluid damage, or every. You must often investigate the fluid while the transmission has clearly run

warm. By routinely, I am speaking about the very next filling station.

3. Set up an outside cooler. In case you discover yourself generally caught in web page visitors, haul a trailer, or regularly haul heavy loads, that might purpose excessive warmth. An outdoor transmission cooler includes the transmission temperature degree down into the everyday jogging range, prolonging your transmissions life.

four. Change transmission liquid frequently whilst the car is applied in excessive-pressure conditions. Your transmission liquid is advanced to chill the transmission and to lube the transmission elements at the same time as providing the hydraulic pressure so all the elements may have interplay. When the transmission fluid isn't always any more capable of carry out those sports activities successfully, the existence of the transmission is notably reduced. In case your automobile runs beneath excessive-stress situations, it is a terrific idea to regulate the transmission beverages instances a yr.

5. Have the transmission linkage inspected and calibrated regularly. This is vital for automobiles underneath a heavy workload.

6. Immediately have malfunctions inspected. Transmission repair art work costs increase in phrases of methods prolonged the auto is driven after the preliminary indicators of hassle. The longer you brush aside a transmission it truly is breaking down, the more you could assume the renovation to value.

7. Ensure your engine is successfully tuned. In case your engine isn't always walking successfully, the symptoms can, in

some times, resemble transmission troubles.

8. Have power train additives regularly examined. There are some pressure educate components which might be linked right away to the transmission working. Universal joints, pressure axles, continuous tempo joints, driveshafts, flywheels, flexplates, computer structures, cooling systems, transmission mounts, engine mounts, and sensing gadgets all make a contribution for your transmission running successfully.

9. Inspect cooling device two instances a 365 days. Have your cooling tool inspected for correct coolant electricity, leakages and degrees. Antifreeze degrades step by step, so it need to be changed to hold its average normal overall performance.

10. Each 365 days have a entire physical carried out on your vehicle. Every 12

months, your car have to be examined from pinnacle to backside, concerning guidance, brakes, lights, and different safety elements.

20 Signs of Potential Transmission Issues

There are all varieties of topics that may get up to transmission, and a number of those preservation can be absolutely expensive. There are a number of signs and symptoms which advise that there is probably transmission troubles afterward. Let's check the top 20 symptoms and symptoms and signs and symptoms.

1. When the car is cold, and also you location it into riding strain, there may be a preserve-up. The car shifts past due at some point of an preliminary short at the same time as of operation.

2. The shifter does not enter into power or contrary. You located the shifter proper right into a the use of pressure (D) or

opposite (R), however in reality not some thing takes location.

3. Fresh discolorations below your automobile.

four. You can not get the shifter to enter any role. Even at the same time as the engine is racing, it does now not budge.

5. Shifting takes region at the wrong pace tiers main to premature or past due transferring.

6. Slippage. The engine rpm is immoderate; but, the auto is going extraordinarily sluggishly, and it does now not boost up.

7. Not capable of area into passing system, or it enters into overdrive, however, there's no rise in power at the same time as you examine the fuel.

8. Rough transferring consequences in a hard sensation or clunking whilst the transmission is located into device.

9. Unpredictable shifting. Velocity, on the identical time as moving takes region, is in no manner ever the equal.

10. There is a burning odor or putrid smell.

eleven. Engine braking does not paintings in numerous positions.

12. The car tries to move whilst inside the park.

13. Service engine light or check moderate keeps coming on.

14. Car stalls at some point of starting off.

15. The shifter signal could no longer element to the first rate tools to any quantity further.

16. The shifter has in fact ended up being tough to move proper right into a characteristic or out of it.

17. You pay attention unusual sounds. Groans, grunts, hisses, and so on.

18. The shifter sign is honestly off independent (N) and/or park (P) at the identical time as you bypass to reveal on the car.

19. When checked, there may be a substantial quantity of filings and particles inside the transmission pan.

20. Shifting all of sudden.

Things You Must Not do if You Wish to Extend Your Transmissions Life

1. Never ever depart your car in the park with out setting your parking brake on. If your car was even absolutely tapped by using way of a few other automobile, it might motive the parking pawl, a element

inside your transmission, breaking, and your vehicle rolling due to that. When ignored, this may bring about extraordinary harm.

2. Never ever brake with the resource of downshifting. It's a regular workout to downshift at traffic lighting in place of making use of brakes. A compelled downshift at a extra RPM bring about vain deterioration on the transmission bands and clutches.

three. Never ever change from energy into opposite even as the engine is at a short idle. This surprising transmission engagement have to result in malfunction of the clutches, bands, equipment sets, driveline elements, in addition to transmission and engine mounts.

4. Do no longer drag race. If your vehicle come to be created for racing, it's miles exceptional. However, inventory

transmissions and drivelines aren't evolved for that kind of abuse or torque, and you'll likely damage your transmission and numerous driveline factors.

5. Never ever rock your car within the sand or snow. Get towed or dig yourself out; however, do now not do this rocking from contrary to electricity which you see many people doing. The more warm temperature which this induces might also need to cause burning your transmission out in a quick time period. A tow is a ways an entire lot less expensive!

6. Do now not drive up until your engine has in fact heated up. For your transmission to be effectively lubed, the fluid has to be at taking walks temperature stage. It might require you a few minutes longer to begin; however, it's far going to spare you a number of cash.

7. Never ever tow your vehicle with the electricity wheels on the floor. Front-wheel strain motors want to have the front wheels in the air. Rear-wheel-strength automobiles need to be hauled with the lower back wheels off the floor. All-wheel or 4-wheel power cars want to be hauled flat. Refer for your proprietor's manual for correct towing instructions to live a long way from vital harm.

eight. Never ever save you all of a stunning. Abrupt stops (and quick starts offevolved offevolved) can purpose damage on your force educate and its elements together with engine mounts and transmission.

nine. Do no longer attempt to restore your private transmission. Nonprescription short fixes which consist of components which is probably advanced to save you leakages or make your transmission shift a good deal better encompass a wonderful deal of severa chemical materials that can set off seals which can be currently used to end up swollen, or they may impact the function of rubber elements which result in greater extreme harm. It does now not pay to play around because of the fact you may prompt extra harm, and the cease very last consequences is going to be a bigger repair fee than what you'll have paid if you had genuinely lengthy lengthy long past to the transmission store.

10. Get normal protection. Ensure your transmission obtains the recurring servicing it requires to stay in excellent form.

10 Sounds that Indicate You Might Have Transmission Issues

Your automobile has conventional sounds which you come to be being used to. When those sounds modify, you may most possibly observe it quite suddenly. If you enjoy a logo-new sound that you have clearly not previously heard, it is probably the start of an difficulty. Here are the primary 10 sounds you need to have a observe out for:

1. Clicking

2. Buzzing

three. Squealing

four. Groaning

5. Screeching

6. Humming in any tools

7. Grating in tools.

8. Clanking even as located into contrary (R) or power (D)

9. Chattering even as placed into reverse (R) or stress (D)

10. Rumbling in tool.

Chapter 15: How to Pick a Mechanic and a Car Repair Shop.

It is hard to undrestand wherein to take your automobile in case you accept as authentic with you require restore art work or renovation. Let's test what you need to look for Experience.

Search for an automobile preserve that has experience. Look period of service and areas of expertise. For instance, in case you require an engine restore paintings, you may choose a mechanics store which has a tune file for first rate paintings. If you require a transmission repair paintings, you then definately would really like to know they're gifted in transmission repair work.

Dependability and Capability

Search for a issuer center with mechanics and professionals who're updated with their education and attending workshops and last modern. You moreover choice to take your automobile to a store which has a music record for being straightforward-- getting the paintings carried out on time.

BBB

It's a terrific idea to offer the Better Business Bureau a name and feature a take a look at whether or not or now not or now not the auto center has without a doubt had any grievances, and in that case, which mechanic and what form of grievances.

Check On the Internet

The Internet affords some tremendous offerings concerning grading automobile mechanic stores. There are message forums, on line boards, net internet sites which fee car repair shops, and so on. There are numerous exquisite belongings at the internet. Make positive to make the most of them.

Request Recommendations

In the event in that you might locate your self coping with a large restore bill, do no longer hesitate to request references from the auto issuer center. In case the garage chooses now not to provide you references, you need to search around some other place.

Look for Accreditation

Ensure the mechanics are certified in relevant areas. Seek to look how many accreditations the mechanic has. The more accreditations, the more in all likelihood it's miles that the mechanic is certainly into what he works on and indicates a authentic hobby.

Ask Lots Of Questions

When you find yourself with a car hassle, do now not hesitate to invite the service creator and/or mechanic questions. You maximum possibly have issues, and also you want to have the capability to collect solutions to make sure that you could with a chunk of success maintain with getting the repair artwork carried out.

There you have got got it. Lots of terrific recommendations to allow you to keep your car searching and walking awesome. These tips are going to move away you with money and time in your hands. Looking after your vehicle indicates you may expect years of problem-free the usage of. What extra can also additionally want to you ask for? An vehicle it surely is dependable, sincere, and prices little to repair is absolutely everyone's dream. These thoughts are going to aid you to get that vehicle.

Chapter 16: Gasoline-powered cars

The conventional gasoline car that you energy nowadays is in fact quite wonderful from the automobile or truck your mother and father drove. Today's vehicles have real laptop structures inner - complete with silicon chips! That approach that at the same time as your vehicle has more features than the ones of preceding generations, it additionally dreams protection to save you highly-priced maintenance as a whole lot as ever earlier than.

Before You Pop the Hood

You can prevent now not brilliant high priced renovation, however furthermore a lethal accident, with the useful resource of way of checking your tires once in keeping with week. Look at all of them to look within the event that they appear similarly inflated. Then, with a tire pressure gauge, take a look at the real stress readings for every tire. You can discover the proper stress reading degree in your owner's guide to your car or tires. Your automobile's tires should be neither beneath or overinflated.

Also, take a look at the wear and tear and tear in your tires through placing a penny in each tire with Abraham Lincoln upside-down and going via you. If the groove of the tire is deep enough that you could't see his face, your tire has ok tread. Once you may see President Lincoln's face, it's time to have the tire changed. If you don't have a Lincoln penny available, stop with the beneficial resource of a tire store and ask them to check the damage and tear and tear on your tires for you.

Also, make a addiction of glancing below your car at a few degree inside the week as you approach it in parking masses. Do you observe any fluids under your vehicle? If you observe small swimming swimming pools of fluid under your car, proper proper right here's an easy way to decide whether or not or not or not it's without a doubt coming out of your automobile: when you arrive domestic, located a chunk of smooth cardboard below the car or truck in a unmarried day. In the morning, a few difficulty your car might be leaking will appear on the card (be aware: inside the summer season, your automobile's air conditioner may also additionally furthermore motive water to drip from the bottom of your car. If the automobile or truck is otherwise performing well, this is normal).

Note while you see coloured smoke coming out of your exhaust pipe - that is a signal of a hassle, whether or not or now not the smoke is white or black, or any colour in among. If you observe any colour of smoke popping out of your exhaust pipe, have a mechanic examine your car right now.

Finally, while you start the ignition, ensure you do no longer see any caution lighting fixtures for your sprint lighting fixtures up. If you do, the ones need to be addressed without delay. The least highly-priced way to discover what that mild manner is to take your automobile to an vehicle factors shop. The personnel now have engine code readers they are able to hook up for your automobile and inform you what the mild suggests (your can purchase the kind of for home use as well. The retail for among $50-one hundred.)

Under the Hood

You need to moreover open the hood and test your vehicle's engine often-as a minimum times in keeping with month.

The first difficulty to test is the oil degree. To do this, find out the dipstick for your automobile or truck's engine (your owner's guide may have a diagram of your engine if you have a trouble locating the dipstick visually). Gently pull it out and wipe it with a paper towel or lint-free rag. Then stick it decrease returned into the oil pipe. Pull it out a 2nd time and check the quantity of the oil - do you've got the amount that your proprietor's guide shows? If not, you could upload greater oil through using pouring greater oil into the place of the most important part of your engine with the oil cap (this is NOT the identical location the dipstick got here out of!). If the oil has particles in it, it wants to be changed.

When your engine is cool (and ONLY whilst it's cool), you have to check the coolant (or antifreeze) stage. To do this, discover the coolant field on your engine (once more, use your owner's manual diagram if wished). The coolant subject has a fill line.

Your coolant degree should be a piece bit over that fill line. If it is, you need now not do away with the coolant cap. If the coolant degree is beneath the fill line, do away with the cap and upload coolant till the volume is barely over the fill line.

The next fluids to check are your strength guidance fluid and brake fluid tiers. These may be checked the identical manner that you checked your coolant levels. Again, if the tiers of those fluids are above the fill line, there's no want to function extra.

The greater regularly you check below your vehicle's hood, the greater acquainted you can get together along with your engine. Within more than one checks, you may be familiar sufficient to be aware whether or not or not your engine's hoses and belts are in proper state of affairs.

Putting air in your tires

At a few point in your vehicle possession, one or greater of your tires will now not have enough air in it. Sometimes you can inform thru simply searching, and one among a type times, your tire pressure gauge tells you this. It is mainly not unusual for your tires to lose air pressure as wintry climate units in, due to the general change in temperature. Adding air in your tires is quite smooth:

1. Air ought to be introduced on your tires at the equal time as they're bloodless, and characteristic most effective been pushed 1-2 miles. Don't air up your tires on the stop of an extended electricity till you need air to get domestic.

2. Check your proprietor's manual for the proper quantity of tire stress in your automobile version.

3. Take your vehicle to the closest gas station (you could use a manual air pump,

but it takes pretty a piece of higher body strength). The air pump is usually on the brink of the parking location - most of the time it's unfastened to clients!

4. Remove the tire's small air cap. Add air via pressing the air pump's head down into the tire's valve, and then pushing the extent at the air pump head down.

five. Once you experience an ok amount of air has entered the tire, cast off the air pump head. Check your tire strain collectively together with your tire stress gauge. If the reading is adequate, update the tire's air cap. If now not, repeat steps 4 and five until you have got were given right enough air pressure.

6. If you flow over the endorsed air pressure, you can launch some air from the tire thru disposing of the air pump head, after which pressing down at the tiny pin inside the center of the tire's valve

stem. Let up on the pin as soon as a few air has flowed out, and take each exclusive studying along with your tire pressure gauge. Repeat this approach if critical.

The maximum vital preservation item

Far and away, the most critical thing you could do for the life of your conventional-fuel vehicle is have the oil and oil clear out modified every five,000 miles (or as frequently as your proprietor's manual directs). The introduced advantage of ordinary oil adjustments is having a second, professional set of eyes in your engine to check for any problem spots.

When you've got your oil modified, ask the mechanics to check your air filter, timing belt, spark plugs and cables.

How to Change the Oil Yourself

Changing the oil in most motors isn't tough, however it's far messy, and you can want some matters to get started:

1. Lift your automobile on a lift or on ramps. Make sure that the emergency brake is engaged and that the ramps are on a totally flat floor.

2. Let your engine idle for two-3 mins so the oil in the engine will warm up without getting too heat. Warm oil will drain extra speedy and any sediment inside the oil is much more likely to drain out than while the oil is cold.

3. While your engine is idling, make certain you have your new oil, a new filter out, a pan and newspaper to capture the draining oil, and probably a socket wrench and a flashlight. Consult your owner's guide to decide the shape of oil and filter you may need.

4. Turn off the ignition and do away with the oil cap underneath your hood. This allows the oil drain out faster.

five. Get below your automobile together with your flashlight and wrench, and function your capture pan internal acquire. Locate your oil pan. It is probably flat and characteristic a plug or bolt on it. If you're now not sure in which it is, take a look at your proprietor's guide diagram.

6. Get your trap pan below the oil plan, then loosen the oil plug slowly. The oil will begin flowing out immediately, and can take several mins to drain thoroughly.

7. Once the drift of outgoing oil has stopped, replace the oil plug tightly with the wrench. Leave the oil pan below the automobile, due to the reality some extra oil may additionally moreover come out at the same time as you convert the oil clear out.

eight. Now, replace the oil clean out: locate your oil clear out collectively with your owner's manual diagram. Unscrew it through turning it counter-clockwise. Make superb the vintage rubber gasket comes off actually with the vintage filter.

9. Smear a touch of your new oil at the rubber gasket of the contemporary day oil clean out (this permits it adhere extra efficiently). Slowly, screw in the new filter.

10. Then, below the hood, upload the modern oil to the oil container, which you however have open. Make sure you wipe up any oil spills off the engine as fine you can, or you may heady scent burning oil while you start the engine.

eleven. Carefully remove the entice pan from below the auto. You will need to test collectively together together with your city or county strong waste branch to appearance the way you want to get rid of the antique oil on your location.You will want to cautiously put the vintage oil into the plastic bottles your new oil came in

12. Start the ignition and decrease back the auto off of the ramp (if relevant). Let the automobile idle for a couple of minutes. If your oil pressure mild comes on, permit the engine run some other little even as to permit the oil warm up (it can then burst off).

thirteen. If the oil pressure mild doesn't flip off, test how constant the oil plug, oil filter out, and oil cap are becoming, and tighten every of them if vital.

Disposing of the antique oil

For many, casting off the vintage oil is greater work than the real oil change, and so it drives many humans to take their cars to oil change shops and allow them to cope with the disposal. If you prefer to trade your own oil, removing it's miles less tough than you can have heard. Here's a way to do it:

1. Pour your antique oil into the plastic bottles your new oil came in. Put the caps on as tightly as viable. Mark the the front of the bottles with permanent marker to alert humans that the ones bottles contain used oil.

2. Take your used oil to a licensed recycling center, it is any area that sells motor oil and/or oil filters (the regulation calls for that companies that promote the ones merchandise recycle oil for their clients). Some metropolis and county strong waste applications will recycle oil - take a look at at the side of your metropolis authorities to look if yours will take the oil, if vital.

Dealing with spilled oil

You don't want to be a multinational oil conglomerate to observe an oil spill and wonder, "How the heck am I going to clean that up?"

But don't worry - it's clean, so long as you have this shape of matters handy:

1. A specialised powder offered at car supply locations for such spills. You can also pay attention it referred to as "oil dry". It's a white powder a good way to remind you of laundry detergent. Keep it out of obtain of youngsters and pets.

2. Kitty clutter. Kitty clutter in truth works simply similarly to oil dry, and it's lots less difficult to maintain reachable. Put sufficient kitty clutter over the oil spill to cowl it from view, and pat it down along side your foot. Let it sit down in a unmarried day. The next day, the spill will look a good deal smaller, and you may sweep up the litter and cast off it as you commonly would possibly any dirty

muddle. You can repeat the approach if critical.

Changing your air clear out

Your air clear out must be modified every 12,000 miles, or as soon as in keeping with twelve months. This is an smooth venture to do your self:

1. Check your proprietor's guide to appearance which version of oil clear out you want (many chain car deliver stores can look it up for you as well)

2. Gently, do away with your vintage filter from its casing below your hood. On maximum cars, the air filter out is held in location with steel clips to hold it firmly in region.

three. Once the vintage clean out is out, gently vicinity the cutting-edge one in place, being super to regular the metallic clips on every facet.

4. You can throw away your vintage air filter out inside the own family trash - no need to take it anywhere unique for recycling.

Tire rotation

Tire rotation is truely what it seems like - shifting each tire to a cutting-edge wheel to your vehicle to make sure even located on. Tire rotation can prevent hundreds of bucks in case you are ordinary about it. Tires should be rotated every 3,000-6,000 miles. Most businesses that promote tires will rotate your tires without rate each 6,000 miles, so maintain your receipt for gadgets of tires to your glove compartment.

Changing your windshield wiper blades

If you ever take a look at the signs inside the home home home windows of chain automobile supply shops, you'll frequently word one that gives free installation with the purchase of latest wiper blades. There is some super print with this signal - this provide is extremely good legitimate with immoderate-give up, greater expensive wiper blades.

Most motorists can perform really notable with price range windshield wiper blades, even though it manner installing them yourself. Most humans want to replace their windshield wipers each 6 months. Here's the manner it's completed:

1. Pull your windshield wipers far from the windshield, as in case you are cleaning the windshield.

2. Inspect the way the vintage wipers are established. Most models have small tabs that release the blades even as driven.

3. Once you have got were given the vintage blades out, you can gently click on on on the brand new blades into place.

Replacing spark plugs

Most cars want to have their spark plugs changed each 30,000 miles (check your proprietor's manual to affirm your vehicle's necessities). Locate them beneath your hood, with huge wires linked to them. Count how many you can need earlier than you buy new ones.

1. DO NOT DETACH ALL OF THE OLD SPARK PLUGS AT ONCE. First, take away the twine from the spark plug closest to you.

2. Remove the spark plug using your spark plug socket and extension for your ratchet.

3. Insert the present day spark plug inside the antique one's region, tightening it at the side of your spark plug socket and extension in your ratchet.

four. Attach the cord.

five. Repeat steps 1-4 for as many spark plugs as your vehicle calls for.

Replacing your tires

Tires are designed to final anywhere from 30,000-eighty,000 miles. That's a huge unfold, so as quickly as you obtain your automobile, have a take a look at the tires and phrase the emblem and model. You can then look up the tires at the net to look how frequently they need to be replaced. Most tires want to get replaced each 50,000-60,000 miles.

With tires now widely available at Wal-Mart car facilities and national chain stores like Goodyear and Discount Tire Company, pricing a modern set of tires is straightforward. Make tremendous that whoever you purchase your tires from offers unfastened tire rotation and restore, and maintain the receipt from your tire purchase in your glove compartment.

Traditional-fuel automobile maintenance precis

• Check your tires and tire stress as soon as normal with week

• Check your engine fluid ranges 2-3 times in line with month

• Change oil each 5,000 miles (or as frequently as your owner's guide directs)

• Have tires turned round each 6,000 miles at a minimum

• Replace wiper blades every 6 months

• Change air filter each 12,000 miles or as quickly as in line with 365 days, whichever comes first

• Change spark plugs each 30,000 miles (or as often as your owner's manual directs)

- Have car tuned as frequently as your owner's guide directs (usually each 50,000 miles)

Chapter 17: Hybrid vehicles

In the past ten years, the assortment of hybrid automobile makes and models has skyrocketed. Without a doubt, hybrid owners keep money on gas. But as we've located out from the preceding bankruptcy, fuel isn't continuously the only manner to maintain in phrases of vehicle ownership. Hybrids have their very private protection concerns that their owners are sensible to be aware of.

Hybrid vehicles are powered from resources, as opposed to first-rate the conventional gas engine - that's why we speak over with them as "hybrids". Hybrids operate as a lot as possible on their batteries, and then switch to the gas engine while important.

Like a Traditional Vehicle

Hybrid vehicle owners have to workout all the easy maintenance conduct listed inside the previous bankruptcy. Also, hybrids need oil changes only a frequently as traditional-gasoline automobiles. You may have the oil modified at all the identical locations you have a traditional-fuel automobile's oil changed.

But Different

Typically, hybrids' batteries have an 8-three hundred and sixty five days or 100,000 mile guarantee. So a ways, hybrid producers show that the batteries are being accurately protected via the ones warranties. The charge of alternative batteries is not posted, and if needed, they will be considerably luxurious (kind of $2,000) till the fee ultimately drops as hybrids turn out to be greater not unusual.

You can also even store coins on brake pads, because hybrid automobiles' braking systems put on a good deal a good deal a whole lot less on the pads than traditional-gas cars.

Barring any unusual problems, a hybrid vehicle will now not want a pinnacle organization for an average of eighty,000 miles - that's greater than many humans located on a vehicle over the time they non-public it.

The cooling tool in a hybrid car wishes a track-up at kind of 100,000 miles, and that is usually greater highly-priced than a cooling tool song-up for a traditional-fuel vehicle. Again, many people received't very personal the hybrid by the point that is required.

The current downside of hybrid vehicles is that you can't take them to certainly any mechanic while there is an trouble - mechanics must be specifically skilled to artwork on hybrids. Right now, maximum of these mechanics art work at dealership restore shops.

So your renovation checklist for a hybrid is type of identical, besides for the song-up you could want after many miles.

Hybrid vehicle renovation precis

• Check your tires and tire pressure as soon as regular with week

• Check your engine fluid tiers 2-three instances according to month

• Replace wiper blades every 6 months

• Change oil each five,000 miles (or as frequently as your proprietor's guide directs)

• Have tires grew to emerge as spherical each 6,000 miles at a minimum

• Change air filter out each 12,000 miles or as quickly as steady with 365 days, whichever comes first

• Change spark plugs each 30,000 miles (or as often as your proprietor's guide directs)

• Have car tuned as regularly as your proprietor's manual directs (usually every eighty,000 miles)

Chapter 18: Electric automobiles

These vehicles are the most attractive idea for those individuals who're indignant by using using the usage of the constantly-rising fee of gasoline: electric powered powered motors take no fuel in any way.

Electric cars, due to the reality they don't require fuel, do no longer want spark plugs, oil adjustments, transmissions, or gas filters. That way an entire lot plenty much less protection than a traditional-fuel car.

Electric automobiles, just like your mobile cellphone, want to be charged. They are greater frequently than now not being charged at home. If you very own a cellular phone or an MP3 participant, that over the years, your battery grade by grade loses its capacity to maintain a complete rate - you need to fee the battery increasingly more often to get the equal quantity of play time. This is the capability hassle with electric powered vehicles.

Right now, a replacement battery percent for a Nissan Leaf (the maximum not unusual electric powered powered powered automobile on the road in 2015) lists for $15,000 - that's nearly the fee of a new electric powered automobile (besides you're in the marketplace for a Tesla, which retails new for about $100,000.

Electric vehicle producers are defensive the proper vehicle battery for one hundred,000 miles. Again, that's extra miles than many human beings placed on their vehicle over the complete time they very own it. Furthermore, the charge of substitute battery packs may additionally moreover come down as electric automobiles become more commonplace.

If this bankruptcy seems truely, actually short, that's due to the reality the upkeep desires on an electric powered vehicle are far fewer than both the conventional-gas or the hybrid automobiles:

Electric car renovation summary

• Check your tires and tire pressure as quickly as consistent with week

• Replace wiper blades every 6 months

• Have tires rotated each 6,000 miles at a minimum

• Change air clear out every 12,000 miles or as soon as consistent with yr, whichever comes first

• Have automobile tuned as often as your owner's manual directs (commonly each one hundred,000 miles)